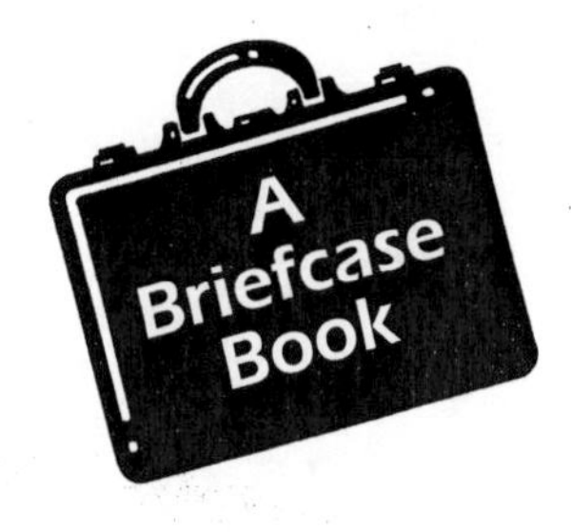

Time Management

Marc Mancini

McGraw-Hill
New York Chicago San Francisco Lisbon London
Madrid Mexico City Milan New Delhi San Juan
Seoul Singapore Sydney Toronto

The McGraw-Hill Companies

13 14 15DIG/DIG 15 14
ISBN 0-07-140610-7

This is a CWL Publishing Enterprises Book, developed and produced for McGraw-Hill by CWL Publishing Enterprises, Inc., Madison, WI, www.cwlpub.com.

This book is printed on recycled, acid-free paper containing a minimum of 50% recycled de-inked fiber.

Contents

Preface

In the 1950s, as home and work chores became increasingly mechanized and as the electronics revolution hinted at an even more startling efficiency to come, futurists made a bold prediction: by the year 2000, the average person would work only 20 or 30 hours a week. There would be so much leisure time that most of us wouldn't know what to do with it.

We now know that these '50s oracles were wrong—very wrong. Electronics and automation have sped up life so greatly that, to keep up with the swift flood of tasks and info-bits, most of us work *more* than 40 hours, not fewer, and have seen our leisure time shrink away. The computer chip didn't free us. It forced us to produce at *its* speed.

So, we're on a responsibility overload. Faxes, Federal Express, and e-mail demand instant action. Computers and laser printers pour out 50 personalized letters in minutes—something that once took a secretary all day to do. Consequently, our mailboxes and in-bins overflow with all sorts of materials that clamor for our attention.

All this communication and the ease of travel mean that the network of people you deal with has grown exponentially. Indeed, you meet more people in one year than your grandparents did in a lifetime. No wonder so many of us have trouble remembering names.

To make matters worse, you may have turned to a book on time management for help before, one that argued (as most do) that you must erect great, logic-based ramparts to hold off the disorganized barbarians or super-efficient competitors out there. The author may have suggested that within those barriers you can reside in a cool, patterned, and neat little environment, practicing the one true religion of time management.

If only it were so easy or true. But you know better.

More often, you feel overwhelmed, exhausted, defeated. You probably even feel guilty taking the time to read one more book on time management—this one. *But there is hope*. That's what this book is all about.

The Right Way and the Wrong Way—Maybe

Tiffany loves computers. She took to them like a duck to water. So when she needs to shuffle among five documents, she finds that the easiest, most effective way to do so is to open five windows on her computer and click among them, going from one document to another, then back again. She can edit them, copy and paste sections from one to another, or combine them into a single document, all with the simple click of a mouse.

Jim, on the other hand, is a pen-and-paper kind of guy. He prefers to lay out hardcopies of the five documents on a worktable and label sections of the various documents for change. He makes notes and additions and repaginates by hand. Sometimes, he even cuts and pastes them with tape into a new sequence. Finally, he types his final draft—or, if he has the luxury, he sends it out to be retyped or edited by someone who really gets computer formatting.

Neither way is necessarily the "right" or "wrong" approach to accomplish the task. Tiffany and Jim have each developed a way of working that accomplishes what they need to do with the least possible stress, in a manner that makes them feel confident and in control.

A good case could be made that using a computerized system is inherently more time saving than a manual approach. But if we require Jim to do his editing on the computer, we may, at the same time, force him into thinking more about the way the computer works than about the job. While Tiffany's instinctive and immediate grasp of the intricacies of word processing enables her to do the job most efficiently, Jim's lack of empathy with the way computer programs operate makes software an "efficiency enemy" for him. Instead of struggling to work out how to format a table, he finds it easier and more satisfying to sketch the table by hand and leave the details of formatting to later—or to someone better equipped for that job.

Of course, we might suggest to Jim that he take classes on the use of the computer. In today's work environment, there's almost no way to be efficient without computer skills. But, by nature, Jim may never become a "natural" like Tiffany. He should certainly try to sharpen his computer skills, but he may never be completely comfortable with them.

And Jim's major talent perhaps lies in a different area. He's most useful to his company not as a word processor but as a business development manager. While he shuffles among those five documents, the company really wants him focusing on their content—not on cutting and pasting electronically while retaining the correct format from one document to another.

It's important to remember, then, while reading *Time Management*, that not every single suggestion, strategy, or technique will work for you. There will be moments of insight when you think, "Yes! Why didn't I think of that?" There will be other moments, however, when you conclude, "I couldn't possibly do that! In fact, I *hate* doing that!"

Be reassured. We are individuals. We learn differently, we work differently, and we succeed using different combinations of methods. Rarely is there a "right" or "wrong" way to organize one's life. *Results* are what matter.

There are, however, many ways to improve upon the systems you already have in place or to consider entirely fresh ones that can make your life—and your job—easier, more productive, and more stress-free. This book, we hope, will provide some useful suggestions to accomplish that. It's up to you to select which strategies are best suited to your particular style of working and which, when incorporated into your routines, will make you more confident in your ability to get the job done—on time, accurately, and with the fewest possible hassles.

But be ready for moments—many moments, probably—when you'll say to yourself, "I've always known that. My *parents* told me to do that!" Sure, but are you *still applying* it? After all, as you'll discover, much of your journey toward better time management is about recommitting to what you already know.

The Benefits of Time Management

Time is finite. We have only so many hours available in a day to live our lives, accomplish the tasks that we need to accomplish, and enjoy our lives.

Every minute we waste in frustration over a task that seems overwhelming is a minute subtracted from the time we've allotted to enjoy life. Even our jobs should provide us with pleasures—a sense of accomplishment, the gratification of recognition for a job well done, and financial rewards, too—that enable us to enjoy our personal lives even more. It can be done. Less stress, more confidence, reduced frustration, greater fulfillment—these are all benefits that flow from leading a time-managed life. Our hope is that *Time Management* will help you achieve all these things and more.

The primary benefit to you, as you read and absorb the lessons here, will be an increase in your on-the-job productivity. But, like other books in the Briefcase Books series, *Time Management* is designed to provide you with far more than that. It's intended to assist you, as well, in helping your frontline staff refine their own time-management skills, in making their jobs easier, and in making them more productive. Even more, it will help you to apply the skills you learn to your life outside the workplace—to your home, your relationships with family and friends—in short, to your life in general.

This sub-theme—that these skills go beyond your own job—will be evident throughout the book. It's interwoven into the content through examples from ordinary life and from the kinds of jobs done by your staff. These examples will serve, we hope, to pique your imagination—to get you to think about other ways to strategically apply the lessons they illustrate. And you'll realize that they can apply in many areas of your own life and the lives of others around you, as well.

This book, as you'll discover, also covers a myriad of other topics that intersect with time management, like organization, efficiency, and goal setting for your personal life. Indeed, time management doesn't exist in a vacuum. It meshes into the very fabric of our daily lives. It goes to the very core of how happy and fulfilling our days ought to be.

So what can you expect as you read this book? In our first two chapters you'll learn about the theories that underpin time management and that can transform, in a fundamental way, how you lead your life. For the rest of the book, be prepared to discover hundreds of practical strategies that will serve you well as you manage your everyday responsibilities.

Special Features

The idea behind the books in the Briefcase Series is to give you practical information written in a friendly person-to-person style. The chapters are compact, deal with tactical issues, and include lots of examples. They also feature numerous boxes designed to expand upon the text's core content. Here's a description of the boxes you'll find in this book.

These boxes do just what they say: give you tips and tactics for being smart in the use of time at work and in your personal life.

These boxes provide warnings for where things could go wrong when you're figuring out how to manage your time.

These books give you specific how-to hints for better managing time.

Every subject has some special jargon and terms. These boxes provide definitions of these concepts.

It's always useful to have examples of what others have done, either well or not so well. Find these stories in these boxes.

This identifies boxes where you'll find specific procedures you can follow to take advantage of the book's advice.

How can you make sure you won't make a mistake when managing? You can't, but these boxes will give you practical advice on how to minimize the possibility.

Acknowledgments

My sincerest thanks to Sandra Williams, my project assistant, and to Karen Fukushima, who provides the quality control for all projects that issue from our company.

About the Author

Marc Mancini's success as a speaker and writer in time management stems in many ways from his immensely varied career activities. A professor at West Los Angeles College, he has taught college-level courses in communications, French, travel, critical writing, cinema, and humanities.

He is also one of the travel industry's best-known speakers, educators, and consultants. It's estimated that over 100,000 travel professionals have benefited from sales and service training programs that he has designed or delivered. Among his clients are Marriott, Holland America, American Express, Lufthansa, and AAA.

Dr. Mancini has authored or produced 12 books, 24 videos, three CD-ROMs, three Web sites, and over 200 articles. His works have been syndicated by the *Los Angeles Times* and *Prodigy*. He has appeared on CNN, ABC's *Good Morning America,* and *Showtime*. He resides in Brentwood, California.

Other titles in the Briefcase Books series include:

Customer Relationship Management by Kristin Anderson and Carol Kerr

Communicating Effectively by Lani Arredondo

Performance Management by Robert Bacal

Manager's Guide to Performance Reviews by Robert Bacal

Recognizing and Rewarding Employees by R. Brayton Bowen

Sales Techniques by Bill Brooks

Motivating Employees by Anne Bruce and James S. Pepitone

Building a High Morale Workplace by Anne Bruce

Six Sigma for Managers by Greg Brue

Design for Six Sigma by Greg Brue and Robert G. Launsby

Leadership Skills for Managers by Marlene Caroselli

Negotiating Skills for Managers by Steven P. Cohen

Effective Coaching by Marshall J. Cook

Conflict Resolution by Daniel Dana

Manager's Guide to Strategy by Roger A. Formisano

Project Management by Gary R. Heerkens

Managing Teams by Lawrence Holpp

Budgeting for Managers by Sid Kemp and Eric Dunbar

Hiring Great People by Kevin C. Klinvex, Matthew S. O'Connell, and Christopher P. Klinvex

Retaining Top Employees by J. Leslie McKeown

Empowering Employees by Kenneth L. Murrell and Mimi Meredith

Presentation Skills for Managers by Jennifer Rotondo and Mike Rotondo, Jr.

Finance for Non-Financial Managers by Gene Siciliano

The Manager's Guide to Business Writing by Suzanne D. Sparks

Skills for New Managers by Morey Stettner

Manager's Survival Guide by Morey Stettner

The Manager's Guide to Effective Meetings by Barbara J. Streibel

Interviewing Techniques for Managers by Carolyn P. Thompson

Managing Multiple Projects by Michael Tobis and Irene P. Tobis

Accounting for Managers by William H. Webster

Taming Time

Have you noticed anything new about news broadcasts? Not long ago, all-news cable stations began to position a scrolling bar at the bottom of our TV screens. The goal: to provide concise "headlines" that go beyond what the on-screen news anchors and correspondents are covering. Programmers now even sometimes add a *second* headline bar to add a layer of text to the scrolling one.

Why do they do this? Because the news now changes so rapidly and the volume of fresh information has become so great that it simply can't be presented any longer within the time constraints of a typical news broadcast. Moreover, many viewers don't have the time to wait for the news. They want it all at once, *now*. Programmers also realize that people have become increasingly able to absorb several streams of information at once. So why not present it that way?

Our lives had begun to reflect a similar change long before this latest approach to communicating news took hold.

Technology has made possible the transmission of increas-

For Example

Making It Up in Volume

The Institute for the Future, Pitney Bowes Inc., and San Jose State University did a study in late 1996 that elicited responses from 972 employees of *Fortune* 1,000 companies. It revealed that workers send and receive an average of 178 messages each day via telephone (24 per day, on average), e-mail (14 per day), voicemail (11 per day), and other mediums. 84% indicated that at least three times per hour their work was interrupted by messages.

And this was in 1996. The numbers today would be *much* higher.

ing amounts of complex data that we need to do our jobs, manage our personal finances, communicate with friends, and organize the ever-expanding volume of information we receive.

As a result, we can be far more productive than perhaps any other generation in history. And we now have the tools—technological, strategic, and personal—that can help us in our efforts to manage our time, enhance our efficiency, and better organize our lives. All it takes is to be open to change and willing to embrace all those new things and ideas that are available to us. We can indeed tame time.

To do so, you must be alert to the challenges that all these changes have generated. For example, when you open your e-mail in the morning, you probably face a blizzard of communications. Some of these are about things you need to know. Many, however, are mere clutter—ads providing information *others* want you to know, but about which you couldn't care less, junk mail that clogs your in-box and demands your time to sort through.

And it's about more than e-mail. Maybe you remember when secretaries handled correspondence, answered phones, screened calls, provided reminders of deadlines and appointments, and helped to prioritize the day's tasks? Today, in many companies, managers sit before their computers, typing their own correspondence, answering their own phones and voicemail messages, making entries in their calendars, and setting priorities without the aid of an assistant. With all of the timesaving attributes of these new technologies, who, after all, needs a secretary? It's just the way things are today. Yes, today's managers sometimes do have administrative assistants. But very often, they're shared among several people.

So these new ways of doing things eat into the time we once devoted to the *content* of our jobs. Like the little razor-toothed monsters in Stephen King's *The Langoliers,* routine responsibilities began eating time.

But there's good news, too. If our responsibilities have increased in proportion to the rate of technological progress, so—in many ways—has our freedom. The same tools that have made you into your own secretary have also provided you with ways of organizing data and creating communications that people only dreamed about 20 years ago. You can quickly e-mail a product photo to a prospective client, create a professional presentation during your lunch hour, and avoid a time-consuming business trip with a simple teleconference.

The new technologies that have blessed us with instantaneous communication and limitless access to information, though, have also brought us the nightmares of even swifter deadlines and work overload. We're working longer hours to manage our increased volume of information and new responsibilities. We're experiencing new kinds of stress. (How did you feel the first time you had to format a table with your word processing software?) And we're facing new kinds of time management challenges.

For instance, the ubiquitous personal computer—long hailed as a time-saving device—has sometimes proven to be just the opposite—a constant demand on our time resources. Voicemail simplifies our lives in some ways, but complicates them in others. Pagers and cell phones keep us in contact with the world no matter where we are—a decidedly mixed blessing when you have a romantic evening planned but are expecting an urgent call. The excuse of being unreachable no longer applies. And a "paperless society"? Paper manufacturers are making more money than ever.

The cost of poor time management skills, then, has risen

For Example

Something to Think About

Imagine a bank that credits your account each morning with $86,400. But, since it doesn't carry over a balance from one day to the next, any money you fail to spend today will be deleted from your account.

What would you do? You'd probably draw out every penny, every single day, before closing time. And—if you're smart—you'd invest some of it for your tomorrows.

Each of us has a bank very much like this imaginary one. It's called TIME.

Every morning it credits you with 86,400 seconds. Every night it writes off, as lost, whatever seconds you've failed to use to your advantage. It carries no balance. It permits no overdrafts. If you fail to make full use of the day's deposit, you lose what you don't use.

Each of us has the same number of seconds to use as we think best, but we don't all use them to best advantage and we don't all invest them wisely.

The clock is ticking. Don't let those precious seconds slip away.

dramatically—and it's measured as much in time as it is in money. We're more conscious of time passing than people were even 25 years ago. It almost seems that we *need* the increased life spans we enjoy today just to squeeze in all the living we want to do.

But we really *can* assert control over those things that eat into our productivity, our leisure time, and our peace of mind. It's largely a matter of being open to change, willing to adapt to new opportunities, and eager to develop and maintain the skills necessary to exert that control. How do you start? By analyzing who you are and your "style" of managing time.

Knowing Your Time Management Style

The preface to this book emphasizes the need to remember that we're all individuals. We do not all work—or even learn—in the same way. Some of us, for example, are *visual* in style: we learn by seeing. Some people, on the other hand, are *auditory* in style, learning and working best through hearing. And still others are *tactile* by nature: they need the sense of touch to fully absorb what they need to know. (Athletes are a prime example.)

We're different in other ways, as well.

Some of us seem to have been born neat. Or childhood experiences, or being born a Virgo, or some other mysterious series of events made us so. Our childhood bedrooms were the pride of our lucky parents, our handwriting was (and remains) neat and tidy, and our sock drawers are perfectly arranged. Others of us are natural clutter magnets, with parents who despaired of getting us to clean our rooms. Today, our desks may vary much resemble the bedrooms of our youth. And some of us are a combination—neat one day and untidy the next, with some parts of our lives elegantly organized and other parts in a jumble.

And some of us are organized in what *appears* to be a wholly disorganized way. Perhaps you're the kind of person who can pull out a sheet of urgently needed paper from the middle of one of a dozen messy stacks in less time than it might take a more obviously organized person to retrieve it from a file cabinet. The *appearance* of disorganization (or organization, for that matter) can be deceiving.

As you learned in the preface, this book isn't about imposing a "one-style-fits-all" approach to managing your time. Your individual style should dictate which suggestions and tips you'll find most helpful. You may also find, however, that your style undergoes a slight—or even major—transformation as you adopt some of the suggestions you'll learn here. If you're the sort of person who never meets deadlines—whose library books were (or still are) always late—you'll most likely *want* to change some elements of your style. If you already manage your time well, you presumably are still open to fine-tuning your approach.

First, though, it's important to understand and acknowledge where you are, right now—today.

Smart Managing

The Value of Time

You may have seen this popular, uncredited e-mail that has widely circulated on the Internet:

- To realize the value of one year, ask a student who failed a grade.
- To realize the value of one month, ask a mother who gave birth to a premature baby.
- To realize the value of one week, ask the editor of a weekly newspaper.
- To realize the value of one hour, ask the lovers who are waiting to meet.
- To realize the value of one second, ask the person who just avoided a traffic accident.
- To realize the value of one millisecond, ask the person who won an Olympic medal.

Time has a value greater than any currency. We may leave our children the money we don't use in our own lifetimes, but we cannot leave them one millisecond of time.

How Time-Managed Are You, Really?

Before you can decide what kinds of changes you want to make—both in your professional career and in your personal life—you need to understand what kinds of choices (many of them subconscious) you're already making. You need to ask yourself some hard questions, delve deeply, and be brutally honest with yourself in answering them. In short, you need a picture of both your natural organizational style and the ways in which that style both supports and undermines your relationship with time.

The First Step

Start by taking a "snapshot" of your time management style. It will be a good first step on the way to understanding your behavior patterns. Check each item you answer "yes" to:

- ❑ Do you have a daily calendar (print or electronic) that you carry with you to and from work?
- ❑ Do you make a copy of every document you sign?
- ❑ Do you have maps in your car? If you don't have a car,

would you keep maps in your car if you had one?
- ❑ Do you usually reconfirm appointments that were made some time ago?
- ❑ Do you try to return a phone call within 24 hours?
- ❑ In your home right now, do you have a customary place for your keys?
- ❑ Do you keep most of your service manuals (e.g., for home appliances, computers, TVs) in a place where you can find them quickly?
- ❑ At home right now, are there a pad and a pencil next to the phone?
- ❑ Is there an official, set time when someone looking for you will find you in your office?
- ❑ If you were to get sick tomorrow, would there be someone who could step in and handle your responsibilities at work with reasonable efficiency?
- ❑ Do you have a filing system at home for your personal papers?
- ❑ If the light bulb in the main lighting fixture in your living room were to burn out tonight, would you have another bulb at home in storage to replace it?
- ❑ Do you ever take with you material to read when waiting to see a doctor?

If you found that eight or more of the above statements could apply to you, you almost certainly have solid management skills. If you identified with 11 or more, that's great—unless your well-organized behavior is obsessive. (More about that in the next chapter.) If you found fewer than eight statements applied, you probably have some work to do.

The Second Step

Now take a close look at the following questions. Check those you would answer in the affirmative.

- ❑ Have you had an unintentional finance charge in the last three months?

- ❑ Do you take work home more than once a week?
- ❑ Do you stay at work beyond your official working hours more than twice a week?
- ❑ While in school, did you frequently cram before a test?
- ❑ Are you presently on a committee that bores you?
- ❑ Do you often put off returning a call to someone you don't like, even if it's important?
- ❑ Do you wait until you have a dental problem to see your dentist?
- ❑ Do you frequently skip breakfast?
- ❑ Do slips of paper with phone numbers, addresses, etc., tend to pile up in your purse or wallet, on your desk, in your pockets, etc.?

These questions assess whether certain deep-seated habits or environmental factors undermine the efficiency of your lifestyle. You might want to reread each question to get a few clues as to where you might need some work. If you have five or more *yes* answers, you need to consider some serious behavioral or environmental reprogramming. And unless you have a score of 0, there are facets of your life that need improvement.

How You Relate to Time

We each have a personal perspective of time, but most of us aren't even aware that we have subconscious feelings about time at all.

Read the following list, then choose five words that you feel *best* apply to time. Allow yourself a little creativity in your choices.

spent	white	friendly
opportunity	lively	unclaimed
exhausting	hollow	ready
busy	handy	effective
mountainous	relentless	tense
valley-like	available	empty
energetic	restless	bumpy
jammed	blank	exciting

How can you interpret your choices?

If you selected valley-like, white, hollow, available, unclaimed, ready, blank, or empty, you view time as something to be filled. On the one hand, this can be positive: you're probably not under very great time pressures. On the other hand, you may be too passive about time, allowing others to dictate its use to you.

If the following terms dominate your choices—spent, exhausting, mountainous, jammed, relentless, restless, tense, or bumpy—you view time as an enemy. This is dangerous. It can mean that you're presently overstressed by environment and responsibilities or that you feel that time controls you. In either case, some change will be necessary before you can truly manage your time.

Did the following words compose the majority of your choices: opportunity, busy, energetic, lively, handy, friendly, effective, exciting? If so, you're the kind of person who takes charge of time, who reshapes it to fit your goals and lifestyle.

What if no one category won? Like many people, you probably have mixed feelings about time. By the time you finish this book, those feelings should change. You should be able to view time as an ally, not as a bully or an enemy.

Your Environment

> Key Term
>
> **Environment** Broadly defined in time management as the major people, places, and things that affect the way people shape their time.

The words *environment* and *environmental* have already appeared several times in this chapter. Environment, in time management, has a broad but defined meaning. It refers to the major people, places, and things that affect the way people shape their time.

Some environmental factors may *seem* beyond your control. What can you do about a spouse who never writes down phone messages? Suppose a color laser printer would simplify your life,

TRICKS OF THE TRADE

Taking Control

Make a list of items and activities that you confront on a daily or near-daily basis. Assign each a numerical value from 1 to 5, with 1 representing an item over which you have no control and 5 an item over which you have complete control.

For example, you have complete control over how you respond to the ringing of your alarm clock in the morning. You also have at least some control over whether or not you answer the telephone when it rings—more control, perhaps, at home than in the office. You may have absolutely no control of morning traffic, but you do have control over your reaction to it.

Begin by attempting to take more control of items you currently value as 4's—that is, not quite complete control, but almost. As you master these, begin with the 3's. And once a month, for the next six months, update your list and your valuations, reevaluating the level of control you're actually able to exert over each item. As you become more conscious of both the need to take control and your power to exercise control, you should begin to see a steady improvement in your "control ratings."

yet you (or your company) cannot afford one? What do you do if your boss is as dysfunctional as the pointy-haired one in *Dilbert*?

We'll examine these challenges in upcoming chapters. Remember: there are clever, subtle ways to conquer almost any obstacle.

In the meantime, you might find it useful to go back to the questions posed earlier and answer them as if you were your boss or your spouse. Then ask yourself these questions:

- Do my answers reflect the true nature of the person I am doing this for, or how I *feel* they are?
- Am I projecting my own values or fears onto them?
- To what extent do their traits affect my business performance?
- What genuine strengths of the other person can serve as an inspiration to me?
- What honest shortcomings of theirs must I find a way around?

- How can I, by example or persuasion, help them grow into better, more time-managed individuals?

If you can identify the ways in which your ability to manage your time is impacted by the behavior of others, it's possible that you can find ways of either changing the behavior of the other person or changing the impact it has on your own life. Even an adjustment in how you view the other person's behavior can change the way in which that behavior affects you.

Where Do the Hours Go?

How many hours do you spend a week watching TV? During which hour do you receive the most phone calls at work? How much reading do you do weekly? Think out your answers before reading ahead.

If you're an average American, each week you watch TV for 25 hours, read for just under three hours, and receive the most phone calls between 10 and 11 a.m.

> **When to Call?**
>
> Smart Managing
>
> Many time management experts advise setting aside a specific hour each day to make and return phone calls. And the very best times to do that are either in the first two hours of the morning or in the last two hours of the afternoon. That's when you'll find most people in the office and most readily accessible by telephone. (If you make calls across multiple time zones, of course, you'll need to factor in the time difference.)

Do these figures match your time utilization? If not, is it because you are *not* typical, or because you under- or overestimated?

Most people have a poorly defined sense of how they spend their time. Even if you have a good sense of how you allocate your time, an inventory of how much time you spend doing various activities may reveal a surprise or two. A very useful diagnostic exercise would be to carry a small notebook with you for a few days and jot down your activities, indicating the time it took you to do each thing. You might want to do this just for your business activities—but you'll find the experiment even more revealing if you include your personal time as well.

An analysis of your time allocation experiment results should include:

- The two most time-consuming activities in your daily *work* life.
- The two most time-consuming activities in your *personal* life.
- The two activities most *surprising* to you in how *much* time they consume.
- The two activities most *surprising* to you in how *little* time they consume.
- An honest appraisal of which activities you feel should consume *less* of your time.
- An honest appraisal of which activities you feel should consume *more* of your time.

The conclusions you draw from this exercise, and from an honest assessment of your time management style, should aid you in identifying those areas of your professional and personal life that could most benefit from change. You may find you need a renewed or decreased emphasis on various factors that affect your time management approach. Or, perhaps, applying more thoughtful time management techniques would be useful to you. You might even decide you need a more comprehensive practice of organizational strategies throughout all phases of your life.

But to achieve any of these things, you must first sweep away some time management myths that may be impeding your progress. That will be the subject of our next chapter.

Manager's Checklist for Chapter 1

- ❑ Technology has provided us with useful time benefits, but also with challenges.
- ❑ With respect to time management, we are all individuals, and we work and learn differently.

- ❑ Your individual style will provide you with clues about the kinds of organizational suggestions and tips that will work best for you.
- ❑ You need to understand how you currently relate to time psychologically, in order to make appropriate behavioral and attitude changes.
- ❑ Self-diagnosis is a critical step in improving the way you manage time.

A Few Myths About Managing Your Time

If you take aspirin after drinking alcohol, you'll never get a headache.
If you read in dim light, you'll eventually go blind.
Water going down a drain in Australia will always flow counterclockwise.

These and other beliefs have so often been repeated that they've taken on a life of their own. Yet each is *absolutely false*. When beliefs are repeated or put into print, they tend to become more credible, even factual.

Such myths seem especially indestructible in time management lore. Worse, they can erode true commitment to an organized lifestyle. This chapter examines the four most treacherous myths that you may encounter as you manage your time.

Myth 1: Time Management Is Just Another Label for Obsessive Behavior

For most people, "obsession" has a meaning that's easy to identify and agree upon: it's an excessive preoccupation with anything. Psychologists define it more precisely. To them, obsessions are persistent and often irrational thoughts that creep into consciousness and are hard to chase out of the mind. Some mild but typical examples: a tune that keeps running through your head, the fear that you forgot to lock your front door, the worry that you left a confidential document on your desk at the office.

When an obsession triggers actions—often strange and of little or no value—this is called a *compulsion*. A classic example from Shakespeare: Lady Macbeth compulsively washes her hands to rid herself symbolically of guilt. To psychologists, Shakespeare's example is telling, for they theorize that obsessive-compulsive behavior is an indirect way of resolving an anxiety or a repressed wish.

Compulsive actions frequently are anchored to time. A few are relatively harmless, though they do generate unwarranted stress. For example, do you really need to know that you can get to work 30 seconds faster by taking an alternate route? Must you save time by *always* working on that flight or commuter train? Do you spend inordinate amounts of time cleaning your desk because you fear the chaos that might result from neglecting it?

A mild obsessive-compulsive, time-related behavior can often be conquered via the six R's:

Are You a Perfectionist?

MISTAKE PROOFING

One of the most common (and pernicious) forms of obsessive behavior—and one that can interfere with true efficiency and productivity—is *perfectionism*. Someone once said, "Perfectionism isn't the solution—it's the problem."

Time management is merely a series of choices—a skill that enables you to differentiate between what you *need* to do and what you'd *prefer* to do. Good organization requires setting priorities, and priorities remind us that time constraints truly do limit our options. Doing a thing well is far more important than doing it perfectly. In fact, the illusion that we *can* do anything perfectly prevents some people from doing anything well at all.

- Raise the behavior to full consciousness.
- Recognize that it produces more stress than results.
- Resolve to try to let go of the habit, since it's clearly counterproductive.
- Realize that if you let it go, it will not be the end of the world.
- Replace it with a behavior that is less stressful but at least as effective as what it supplanted.
- Repeat the new pattern until it becomes neutral, relaxing, and accepted.

Individual, isolated, obsessive actions are not always the problem. More common is a general overemphasis on the importance of time. Indeed, in lay terms, this is what obsessiveness is all about. It conjures images of a person who uses a blender to avoid chewing, who wants to watch *60 Minutes* in 30 minutes, who is, deep down, either frantic or a workaholic.

Everyone, at one time or another, gets obsessive about time. Here are some examples:

- People who feel guilty when they do nothing productive on the weekends.
- People who stay at work beyond their official work hours more than once a week.
- A person who tries to arrive exactly on time—neither early nor late—for appointments.
- A driver who is upset by red traffic lights.
- Shoppers who get upset when the other line at the supermarket checkout stand moves faster than theirs.
- People who (a) subscribe to more than six magazines and (b) feel guilty if they throw one away unread.
- A person who dreads vacations because work won't get done back at the office.
- People who lose their temper at work more than they'd like to.
- People who, when alone at home, pick up the phone when it rings, even if they're busy doing something important.

Of course, we've all been guilty of these behaviors at one time or another. Don't worry if you recognize yourself in a few of these. But what if many of these behaviors are common for you? Five or more of these indicators signal an obsessive "danger zone." You should be alert to an overcommitment to time and your perceptions of its requirements. And be aware that figuring out the most time-efficient solution is not always feasible. Here's a quick example. An obsessive salesperson is going on a short, five-city trip and wants to figure out *the* most efficient solution. Bad news: mathematically, there are 120 ways this trip could be scheduled. So remember, settle for a very good solution, not *the* best.

Stress from the Outside

Not all stress comes from internal, unwarranted, and obsessive feelings. Real factors exist that pressure you into that familiar feeling of being overwhelmed. This seems especially true in today's technologically enhanced society, where information overload has created a virtual tidal wave of responsibilities for most workers. Often, these lie beyond our control. In fact, this lack of control represents the single most important factor contributing to stress.

Since people react differently to stressful situations, it's

> CAUTION!
>
> **What Creates Stress?**
>
> A well-known "social readjustment scale" was devised that gave points for various stress-causing events. Death of a spouse was rated highest (100 points), followed by divorce (73), marital separation (65), and a jail term (63). Tellingly, some of the occasions for stress mentioned in this list are, in theory, positive events, such as retirement (45), marital reconciliation (45), or a vacation (13).
>
> Though this scale is useful and often insightful, it does have a problem: it treats everyone the same. Some people shrug off stressful events—both negative and positive—as if they were minor inconveniences. Others have a hair-trigger response to them. Still others may be seriously affected by negative events, but are able to experience positive ones as "de-stressing."
>
> Which are you?

important that you understand the degree to which you're vulnerable to stress. Studies show that people who are the least vulnerable to stress tend to exhibit the following characteristics:

- They have many friends and acquaintances.
- They eat regular meals.
- They sleep well.
- They drink alcohol sparingly.
- They don't smoke.
- They exercise regularly.
- They rarely drink coffee.
- They're affectionate.
- They feel comfortable with the amount of money they make.
- They're in good health.
- They gain strength from their spiritual beliefs.
- They're open about their feelings.
- They belong to at least one club or social group.
- They are neither overweight nor underweight.

It's important to note that if some of these healthy characteristics don't apply to you, you can change. You can decide to exercise more, smoke less, cultivate friendships, and avoid skipping meals. And, if you do, you'll be armoring yourself against those stressful forces that often are inevitable. And remember: time management can serve as a sturdy, second shield to parry many of life's pressures.

Type A—and Type M—Behavior

Several decades ago, a group of researchers noticed certain psychological patterns in people who were prone to disease—especially heart disease. They labeled the syndrome *"Type A" behavior.*

Since then, a great deal more has been learned about Type A behavior, including that such behavior is not quite as simple as people once believed. One lasting insight emerged, though: that aggressive, hostile reactions to threats—perceived or actual—are at the core of Type A behavior.

A good many of the satellite tendencies of a Type A personality have to do with time. Type A people set unreasonable schedules—for themselves and for others. They establish impossible or inappropriate goals. They cram everything into the last minute. They have little time for friends. And, interestingly, even though they seem in constant, frantic activity, they rarely seem to get anything done. Type A's boast of their frenzied carryings-on, seek out your sympathy, or try to impose their style on you. They're prophets of zoom.

On the other hand, there are people who are virtually reverse, mirror images of a Type A. Let's call them Type M. They're quiet but commanding achievers. Their goals are reasonable, their schedules balanced, their dispositions even-tempered. Colleagues and friends admire them for getting things done. And they seem to suffer less from the recurring ills that plague the classic Type A, as shown below:

Type A	Type M
Unreasonable schedules	Reasonable schedules
Unreasonable goals	Reasonable goals
Cramming behavior	Long-range planning
Aggressive, hostile	Relaxed, understanding
Mostly acquaintances	True friends
Frequently ill	Generally healthy
Frantic activity	Steady achievement
Rarely get things done	Get things done

The bottom line: you should strive to replace as many Type A traits as you can with Type M ones. It's the reasonable—and healthy—thing to do.

Myth 2: Time Management Extinguishes Spontaneity and Joy

The preceding discussion should serve to convince you of the hollowness of this myth. Time-managed people set aside whole blocks of time for life's pleasures. They know that certain things need to be organized and others do not. It is the poorly time-managed who—because of disorganization, stress, and foggy priorities—lose the fun in life. And time-managed people can still profit from something that they could not have expected or planned.

Indeed, sometimes our most productive ideas come to us in moments of spontaneity or play. People who have a firm control of their time are able to realize the joy that may come from a spontaneous moment. And they can recognize an unanticipated opportunity when they see one.

If you haven't engaged in at least two of the activities you find most enjoyable within the past month, you need to learn to manage your time to enable you to do so, regularly, in the future. Those who fail to find ways to take advantage of life's joys prove to be less effective in their work environment than those whose lives are more well-rounded—despite the overcommitment of hours they allot to their jobs.

The same thing is true of work itself. It's important to pursue, among other job-related goals, the goal of doing work you enjoy and feel motivated to perform. One study concluded that the problem in America has rarely been high *un*employment—rather, it has been high *mis*employment. What this really means is that many people work in jobs that give them no pleasure and for which they're temperamentally unsuited.

CAUTION!

Karoshi

In Japanese, this term means "death by overwork," a syndrome that purportedly claims at least 75-100 lives a year in Japan. Studies indicate that of the 8,760 hours in a year, *karoshi* victims worked in excess of 3,000 hours during the year prior to their death. As a service to their employees, one Japanese company even provided actors who would visit the aging parents of overworked adult children too busy working to visit their parents themselves.

Though few of us should fear *karoshi*, we should be especially careful not to allow overwork to drain energy and meaning from our lives.

This is especially dangerous if you're a manager—because you often lead by example. If you seem to enjoy your job, it'll be easier for your employees to achieve satisfaction in what they do. Conversely, if you seem burned out, those you manage almost surely will see their motivation erode.

Good time management should include finding the time to pursue work-related goals, the ones that you believe will bring you satisfaction and that involve activities you find stimulating. Productivity isn't merely a function of hard work and time—it involves a psychological commitment to your work as well. We're at our most productive when we enjoy what we're doing, when we have confidence in our abilities to do the job well, when we can react spontaneously to unexpected opportunities, and when we're not distracted by the sneaking suspicion that we should be doing something else.

Myth 3: Maybe I Can Organize Myself, but My Company Can Never Organize Itself

It's easy to be cynical about one's own company. Its size, perhaps, seems to encourage inertia. Since you see the business from within, every flaw is both magnified and clearly defined. But there's hope. It *is* usually possible to find ways to minimize how certain kinds of systemic disorganization (and the poor time management it abets) will affect you. The key to coping with the dysfunction around you is, whenever possible, to take control.

Many people believe that it's impossible to control their work environment or they're afraid of trying to exert control. After all, the act of taking control often involves additional responsibilities and duties. Sometimes, people fear failure or feel that accepting more responsibility will just make a situation that already seems overwhelming worse. But studies regularly show that—regardless of position within a company—the more control a person has over how he or she exercises his or her duties and over the kinds of responsibilities he or she may have, the more satisfying that person's job and life become.

There are many ways of taking control of one's situation.

Here's an example.

A manager working in a highly disorganized and unproductive position within an airline learned she was about to be laid off. Encouraged to apply for another position within the airline, she found a managerial job opening in the cargo division. Even though she recognized that she knew little about cargo and that making a change would require learning new skills, she also knew that the division was highly regarded—efficient, well staffed, and less stressful. She applied for the position, and got it.

A year later, she found that she was delighted with the change she had made. She was now working in a proficient and well-organized department, surrounded by efficient and productive people, and able to exercise her own considerable organizational skills with far fewer obstacles and less stress. Change, she discovered, wasn't as bad as she had feared. In fact, it led to a far more gratifying work situation.

Changing jobs isn't always possible, though. So what do you do when faced with inefficiency and disorganization in your immediate work environment? The best approach—although apparently counter-intuitive—is to investigate ways to assert some control over that environment itself. For example, you might suggest to a well-placed ally that you'd be willing to serve on a committee to create a better distribution of responsibilities within your division. (If you can arrange to chair the committee, even better.) You at once take control of the agenda, help shape the process, and are able to delegate responsibilities. By exerting some control over the process, you'll perhaps create a better situation for yourself.

Other possible ways of achieving control over your work environment:

- If you have problems with constant interruptions during your workday, ask permission to work more flexible hours or even telecommute on certain days.
- Arrange to travel more on business. Much useful work can be done on an aircraft or in a hotel room, without the distractions usually associated with telephones and office

doors. (On the other hand, if you find travel highly stressful, then this solution would be inappropriate.)

- Make individual arrangements for the best ways to communicate with the people you work most closely with. For instance, ask that your co-workers provide you with one hour a day in which they won't telephone or walk into your office, except in a dire emergency.
- If one of your problems is that other people constantly misplace documents, be sure to make a backup copy of all current documents requiring the attention of others.
- If you have problems getting other people to meet their deadlines, consider dividing the work up into smaller pieces, with mini-deadlines for each piece. Some people work best by concentrating on a tree rather than the entire forest.

Of course, some forms of environmental disorder will be outside your control, no matter what you do. Different companies have different cultures. If your way of working deviates from that of the culture of your company, you have only two choices: adapt to the rhythms and style of that organization or look elsewhere for a company where you'd feel more comfortable. Remember, too, that it's always possible to be an island of calm in a sea of confusion, if you take control—at the very

MISTAKE PROOFING

Use Your Imagination

Did you know that in some cultures there's no word for "hour" or "minute"?

Presumably, your company isn't one of them. In response to a survey question, "Do you feel that you have enough time in your daily life?" 90% of respondents admitted to a sense of "time poverty." You aren't alone.

One way to encourage your company—particularly if it's small—to adopt a more balanced view of time might be to suggest a monthly (or even weekly) "down time" hour—one hour when employees turn off their computers and congregate in a room without phones for coffee and pastry and chitchat—no work-related subjects permitted!

least—of your *own* area of responsibility.

Myth 4: One Style Fits All

This book's preface emphasized a crucial point: we are all different. Your goal should be to arrive at a time management style that suits *you*. Some strategies apply to most people in most situations (like setting priorities, planning ahead, delegating), but others require an angle that's tailored to the personal style of the individual. Unfortunately, most time management books and systems seem oblivious to this. They assume that one style fits all.

Experience teaches us that this is far from being true. For example, given the option, you may like to work completely through one project and complete it before moving on to the next: you work in linear fashion. Or you may be holistic in your approach: you enjoy juggling multiple tasks at the same time—like those plate spinners who somehow manage to keep seven or eight disks spinning simultaneously on top of tall poles.

You may also be a "sprinter": you work in great, short bursts of energy and need to recharge your batteries with moments of low activity or rest. On the other hand, you may be a cross-country type: you burn less brightly—but more evenly—throughout the day. (More about this in Chapter 5.)

The bottom line: you should feel comfortable about tailoring your time management style to your psychological and physiological makeup. Of course, this isn't always possible. But the simple recognition of your individuality—and the knowledge that time management principles aren't always carved in stone—can smooth your transition to more efficient, productive, and stress-free performance.

Time Management and Culture

The "Western Way" is hardly the only way to deal with time. Yet, virtually every time management book, by omitting cultural factors, seems to imply that there's one, almost saintly way of doing things. This omission seems nearsighted, considering the

Cultural Perspectives

There are 20 blackbirds sitting in a tree. You shoot one with a slingshot. How many are left?

A typical "Western World"—almost reflexive—response will be "19, of course." But ask, say, a traditional African tribesman the same question and his response—likely to be equally reflexive—would more probably be "None."

And, of course, he'd be right. The remaining 19 are no longer sitting in the tree; they've flown off. To this traditional African, the need for interaction and the instant communication of danger among the birds would be obvious.

Much of what we term the "Western World" applies a kind of knee-jerk rationalist perspective to all problems—even those which would be better addressed by a more intuitive or interpersonal approach. The "truth" about any situation may be more complex and have more components than our own sometimes narrow cultural reflexes would suggest.

following factors:

- If you do business with foreign companies, familiarity with their attitudes toward time and other cultural values will smooth the way to lucid and efficient communication.
- If your boss or a colleague comes from another country, you may be better able to anticipate his or her expectations.
- If you supervise a multicultural work force, you'll gain insights into your employees' ideas of efficiency and can help them to adjust to the time and/or cultural environment that they're now working in.

Time management is deeply embedded in culture.

Type 1: Linear	Type 2: Overlapped
One task/person at a time	Many tasks/persons at a time
Precise schedules	Loose schedules
Punctual	Unpunctual
Clearly stated goals	Goals often unstated
Task oriented	Socially oriented

Active	Relaxed
Structured	Flexible
Socializing at work is discouraged	Socializing at work is common
Business starts, ends early in day	Business starts late morning, ends late
Efficiency valued	Efficiency less important than people
Procedures, routines clearly defined	Procedures, routines not fully defined or followed
Examples	**Examples**
United States	Africa
Canada	Middle East
Germany	Latin America
Switzerland	Southern Italy
Scandinavia	Greece

Researchers have identified two global approaches to time, as shown below and continued on the next page:

It's extremely important to realize that these are *general* traits that characterize time behavior in a *majority* of cases. Exceptions exist in any culture. You should avoid stereotyping, but remain alert to these time management patterns that exist in a general way.

These patterns, too, are in constant flux. Many formerly linear types in the Western World are learning to overlap activities through multitasking in the same way as people in "developing" countries. And some countries or regions represent a blend of both styles. Australians, for example, tend to be well scheduled and organized, but they do put a premium on socializing and are more flexible than most. Residents of Hawaii have a thick veneer of U.S. linear thinking, but underneath lie the old, relaxed ways of native "Hawaiian time." The Japanese exhibit a unique mix of both overarching trends: punctual, organized, and efficient, they nonetheless invest huge amounts of initial time on socializing in business situations. Their goals are usually clearly set but are unwritten and unspoken.

Also keep in mind that time expectations differ even within a country. Someone from a metropolis such as New York thinks very differently about time than does someone from little Seekonk, Massachusetts. A person from the Midwest embraces different values about chronology than one from the Northeast.

Who's to say that any one style is better than another? Americans who visit Italy often go crazy at the inefficiency, while Italians argue that Americans are obsessed with things and organizations, rather than people.

Even corporations themselves have individual "cultural" attitudes about time. Within some companies, a more casual and less hierarchical culture may place a higher value on creativity than on efficiency. Many high-tech firms depend more on research and development—on nonlinear ways of thinking—than do more traditional kinds of businesses.

The key is to adjust to another culture's style, to help others adapt to yours, and to find strength within your own cultural systems while remaining open to borrowing from others.

Like the other myths about time management, believing that only one style fits all is self-defeating. On the other hand, accepting that you can manage time within the framework of your own personal style may liberate you to find the joy in a well-organized life and overcome the barriers that may be keeping you from achieving success you deserve at managing time.

Manager's Checklist for Chapter 2

- ❑ Myths about time management can erode true commitment to an organized lifestyle.
- ❑ Time management is *not* merely a label for obsessive behavior.
- ❑ Time management is, in part, a tool for stress reduction, both in the workplace and in one's personal life.
- ❑ Rather than stifling creativity and pleasure, time management can, in fact, create opportunities for them.

- ❑ What you learn about time management can help you make real and effective changes within your company.
- ❑ Individuals have different time management styles. One size does not fit all.
- ❑ Insight into cultural differences in relation to time can both provide new ideas for time management and help with adapting to unfamiliar ways of doing things.

Lining Up Your Ducks: Prioritize!

"Lining up your ducks" is a familiar and charming phrase. It derives from the tendency of baby ducklings to swim in a perfectly straight line behind their mother. If the ducklings begin to stray too far, the mother duck will invariably "shepherd" them back into line—thus, "getting her ducks in a row."

The application of this phrase to time management is clear. If you deal with things in a logical, orderly sequence, you're sure to bring efficiency and results to your efforts. When your "ducks" begin to stray too far afield, danger is lurking—for them and for you.

Want a winning game plan for your life? This chapter will help you create it. It will examine prioritizing in all its forms: short term, long term, personal, professional, and more. It will guide you through a revealing array of possibilities. And it will expose you to five prioritizing options from which you can choose. The goal: to find a ranking process just right for your style and disposition.

The ABC System

Preached by virtually every time management expert (especially time guru Alan Lakein) and practiced by more organization-sensitive people than any other method, the ABC system is the "grandfather" of prioritizing strategies. In a nutshell, it says that all tasks can—and should—be given an A, B, C value:

- A tasks are those that *must* be done, and soon. When accomplished, A tasks may yield extraordinary results. Left undone, they may generate serious, unpleasant, or disastrous consequences. Immediacy is what an A priority is all about.
- B tasks are those that *should* be done soon. Not as pressing as A tasks, they're still important. They can be postponed, but not for too long. Within a brief time, though, they can easily rise to A status.
- C tasks are those that can be *put off* without creating dire consequences. Some can linger in this category almost indefinitely. Others—especially those tied to a distant completion date—will eventually rise to A or B levels as the deadline approaches.

> For Example
>
> **Huh?**
>
> Perhaps the manager who wrote the following memo might like to rethink his or her priorities: "Doing it right is no excuse for not meeting the schedule."

There's one additional category that you might like to use, if you feel that three are really not sufficient to cover all your bases:

- D tasks are those that, theoretically, *don't even need to be done.* They're rarely anchored to deadlines. They would be nice to accomplish but—realistically—could be totally ignored, with no obvious adverse or severe effects. Strangely, though, when you attend to them (often when you have nothing better to do), they can yield surprising benefits. A few examples: reading an old magazine that turns out to contain a valuable article, buying a new reading lamp for your desk that improves your work environment dramatically, browsing through a stationery store and discovering an organizational tool that will make your filing much easier, or rereading your cell phone instructions to find out some wonderful functions you never knew it had.

The beauty of the ABC system is that it helps strip away the emotions we have about each task. Maybe the last thing you want to do is your expense report, but giving it an A priority the night before might be just what you need to get past your distaste for the process.

The ABC System in a Nutshell

TOOLS

To summarize, here are the tasks the letters represent:

- A tasks: Critical and time-sensitive
- B tasks: Important, but slightly less time-sensitive than A Tasks
- C tasks: Not time-sensitive—yet
- D tasks: Optional—nice, but neither important nor time-sensitive

For some, even the ABC system remains too constricting. Or it spawns too many A's or C's. In this case, you may wish to subdivide even further: A1, A2, A3.

Applying this system to your own situation should help to give you a clearer sense of how it works. Make a list, for example, of 10 things you would *ideally* like to accomplish tomorrow. Then select from this list four items that you *really* expect to do, ranking them in order of importance. The first two will be A tasks and the second two B tasks. Now, from your list of 10 choose two more items that will probably be on your mind tomorrow but can be put off, if necessary. These are C tasks. The remaining four items are most likely D tasks: nice to do but in no way pressing. You might do them tomorrow if you have nothing better to do and feel ambitious or motivated.

This little exercise can reveal clues to your behavior—both actual and ideal.

- Did the first random list reveal a logical progression of activities or how your responsibilities feel to you? What

What's Important?

Smart Managing

How do you decide the relative importance of various tasks? Below are five criteria by which you can weigh tasks when assigning them priorities:

1. High payoffs. Which tasks will provide the best return on investment for your time and energy?
2. Essential to your goals. Which tasks are absolutely critical for meeting personal and professional goals?
3. Essential to your company's goals. Which tasks will most benefit your company, providing it with the best return on investment for employing you?
4. Essential to your boss's goals. Which tasks does your boss regard as most important?
5. Can't be delegated. Which tasks can be done only by you? These will be high priorities.

The best time to set priorities is the afternoon or evening before—not the morning. That way, you can sleep on your priority list and then review it in the morning. You may spot some things you want to change.

does this tell you about the way you think?

- Did the A, B, C importance list produce duties in the order that you're most likely to do them? If not, why not?
- Are you putting off an A1 priority because it's unpleasant? Might it be better to do it first thing and get it out of the way?
- Will you be getting to your C priorities soon? If not, why not? Why were they on your mind? Will they soon become A's or B's?
- Are there any D priorities listed that you would really like to get done? Do you have a block of time soon that you could set aside for them?
- Is tomorrow a workday? If so, what *personal* A's, B's, C's, and D's might you have formulated if tomorrow were *not* a workday? How many of these would include family, friends, personal goals, or just plain loafing?
- Conversely, if tomorrow is a day for personal matters,

what might you have written if it were a workday?

As you ponder these questions, your responses may lead you to insights and spark the will to prioritize things differently. You may even wish to create a personal set of criteria for deciding which items really belong in which categories.

The ABCs of Prioritizing

These approaches can facilitate your prioritizing:

- Label every task you list in your organizer with a letter value. An assumption: you have some sort of organizer, either electronic or paper. (More about this indispensable tool in Chapter 10.) Just doing this may prompt you to rearrange the time order of some of the things you have "penciled in."
- Fill out a to-do list in random order, then label each item with a rating. This list should drive your scheduling.
- Equip your desk with a three- or four-tray filing system. Label the top tray the A tray, the next down the B tray, and so forth. Place each project, etc., in a folder and file it in the appropriate tray. (Some computer programs allow you to do this with electronic files.) Every morning, review the A's and B's, moving items up as needed. Check through the C's and D's every Friday morning to detect tasks that you need to move up.

Smart Managing

Is It Critical or Urgent?

This important distinction, when assigning priorities, is a matter of time. A task is *urgent* when it must be done *immediately*. Such a task may be less important, in the long run, than other, more *critical* (that is, extremely important) tasks, but its importance is magnified by the fact that it's extremely time-sensitive. So it's always *critical* to schedule *urgent* tasks first, even if the importance of the task (all other things being equal) would make it a B rather than an A.

The Index Card/Post-it® System

If you prefer a more user-friendly system for putting your tasks in order, try this paper-based variation of the ABC system. Write each of your duties on a separate index card. Lay the cards out on a flat surface; then place them in order of importance or needed action. You can also do the same with large Post-it® notes. You need not even place them on a horizontal surface: you can arrange them in rows on the wall. You can also use large magnetic boards that allow you to move tasks around easily.

These systems of prioritizing have two considerable advantages. First, they permit a *team* of people to prioritize, because a number of people can, at once, see and manipulate tasks. Second—and more important—they enable you to see at a glance, without rummaging around on your desk for a list, exactly what your next task should be, saving a few moments of your precious time.

TOOLS

The Tickler File

A slightly different version of the index card system involves keeping a tickler file. Number 31 individual file folders, each with a day of the month, and place them in hanging files (or use an expandable file folder with 31 slots). Put each task you need to complete into a file folder, based upon its time-sensitivity. For example, if you need to pay a bill by the 25th, place it in the folder labeled the 19th or 20th. The more time-sensitive an item, the earlier in the file it should be placed. If an activity must be done *on* a given date, it should be placed in the folder of the *day before* as a reminder, then moved to the correct folder when read. Anything you must work on today and tomorrow should be moved from today's folder at the end of the day. Always prioritize a day's folder late in the afternoon of the previous day.

Electronic versions of date-driven tickler files have become a mainstay of many businesses. If you must deal with something paper-based (e.g., a property tax bill), then enter a *reference* to that bill in your computer program's tickler file (e.g., "Pay the property tax").

The Inventory System

Another variation of the ABC approach—the inventory system—is primarily *results*-oriented. Rather than having A, B, C values drive your activity, the inventory approach assumes that you learn the most by reviewing how you handled the day, then applying what you learned to the next day's behavior. It argues that post-activity analysis represents a more realistic, behavior-changing, feedback-oriented approach to dealing with life than does value-seeking.

Evaluating the relative productivity of each day's activities is central to this system. It's important to establish at the beginning what you hope to accomplish, then compare that with what you *actually* accomplish, to get an idea of how successful your current methods are and what kinds of changes would improve current practices.

While this method is not, in itself, a time-saving measure, it can *generate* time-saving behavioral changes. As you discover what activities are more productive and efficient, the theory goes, you'll begin to adjust your behavior accordingly. And as you do so, you'll start to shave wasted minutes off your schedule. Behavior modification is a significant time management strategy. If you practice the inventory system with the intention of altering your behavior according to what you learn from it, the result will almost certainly be time better spent.

The Payoff System

"What's the payoff?" Stephanie Winston, author of *Getting Organized* (New York: Warner Books, 1991, revised), asserts that this is *the* essential question to ask yourself when you begin to prioritize.

The payoff approach certainly fits well into a long tradition of viewing time as a sort of currency. "Time is money," declared Benjamin Franklin over 200 years ago, when the leisurely pace of rural America still dominated life. Now, with the flood of infor-

Key Term

WIIFM "What's in it for me?" A familiar term in both management and sales, WIIFM is the element that always motivates a purchase or a conceptual "buy-in," and it's essential to motivating almost anyone to do anything.

When motivating yourself to change behavior, you should always find a way to clearly express the WIIFM. Writing it down is the very best method of being certain that you've identified the benefit(s) you'll receive from making the change. Without an acknowledged benefit—a fully expressed WIIFM—it's almost impossible to alter your behavior.

This applies, too, to those you may manage. From the start, convey the WIIFM of any assignment and you won't waste time later explaining why something should be done.

mation, duties, and events that overwhelm people every day, time has become a far more valuable commodity. To treat your use of time in terms of financial value and return makes eminent (and measurable) sense. After all, people *spend* time, don't they?

As an example of how this system works, the imaginary tasks listed below represent a spectrum of "value" that extends from having a "high payoff" to a "low payoff." The yield may not always be financial, because there are many other kinds of value to consider here: emotional, social, practical, pleasurable, and so on. Think about how you'd view each: high payoff, medium payoff, or low payoff:

- Get $200 from an ATM—you're down to $20.
- Write a complaint letter to a hotel chain.
- Organize your home office area.
- Pay bills that are due.
- Return a call from a charity you don't want to give to.
- Shop for a new refrigerator.
- Listen to your spouse excitedly tell you about something that really doesn't interest you.
- Talk a neighbor into co-building a fence between your properties.
- Go grocery shopping for the family dinner.
- Return three phone calls from friends.

- Read a magazine article about Hawaii. You're thinking of vacationing there.
- Go to an evening seminar on personal financial planning. You're not signed up yet.
- Listen to your teenage daughter complain about not getting along with her friends.
- Return a call from someone you don't know. (You don't know what it's about, either.)

It wasn't easy to prioritize this imaginary list, was it? This brings home the fact that your emotional reactions and the context of each action affect your decision.

As we said, however, *scheduling* needs to be logical. While you may think at first that grocery shopping is a higher priority than going to the ATM, if you need the cash to purchase the groceries the ATM becomes the higher priority. If completing one task depends upon first finishing another task, the latter task takes on a greater priority—even if, from a seemingly objective viewpoint, it's minor. And just because you'll enjoy reading a magazine article on Hawaii doesn't mean that you should do it first.

This imaginary list of personal tasks can translate just as easily into work-related ones. Sometimes the "payoff" is obvious. At other times, the WIIFM may not be so evident. To return to a previous example, you may at first perceive no benefit to you from volunteering to chair a committee to improve employee-employer relations at your firm, but the solutions that

Uh-Oh

MISTAKE PROOFING

A magazine ran a "Dilbert Quotes" contest a few years ago, soliciting real-life examples of Dilbert-type management. The winning example was from a Microsoft employee who cited a memo that outlined the following procedure:

1. Beginning tomorrow, individual security cards will be required to enter the building.
2. Next Wednesday, employees will have their pictures taken.
3. Security cards will be issued two weeks later.

emerge from that committee might have an effect on you personally, should problems arise between you and your superiors.

It's surprising how often people can be neat and orderly in their business life but rumpled and disorganized in their personal life. Sometimes it can't be helped—family members can alter your behavior in ways that business colleagues cannot. Still, the payoff system seems especially good at illustrating how the principles of business conduct can furnish strategies to improve your personal life and vice versa.

One last payoff thought: how much do you make, in dollars and cents, per hour? From now on, when you find yourself truly wasting time—or letting someone else squander your time—think of that hourly figure and how the value of your time is slipping away. Both you and your company benefit from the most efficient use of your time. And you can measure that value in actual monetary terms. In fact, your raise may depend upon it.

TRICKS OF THE TRADE

"Not-to-Do" Lists

Author Michael LeBoeuf offers a fascinating idea that may serve to free the spirit as well as some much-needed time. His idea: create a "not-to-do" list, which he believes should include the following kinds of items:

- All low-priority items, unless you've successfully completed all your high-priority items.
- Anything you could reasonably delegate to someone else.
- Demands on your time from others that are either thoughtless or inappropriate.
- Any errand that, if ignored, will have minimal consequences.
- Anything you might have done for someone else that the person should be doing for himself or herself.

There's a kind of exhilaration in setting down on paper a list of things you're not going to do. You can mentally tote up the minutes you're going to save by not doing them. The sense of freedom that this little exercise engenders can work wonders on the subconscious and can even lower your level of stress.

The Pareto Principle

Certain numbers (like pi) and shapes (such as the hexagon and the spiral) somehow recur in nature. They seem to underlie the fabric of reality itself, in ways that remain largely incomprehensible, even to scientists and mathematicians.

Time management, too, harbors something that surfaces with mysterious regularity: the 80/20 formula, also called the Pareto Principle. An Italian economist, Vilfredo Pareto, observed in 1906 that 20% of Italians owned 80% of that nation's wealth. Over time, this ratio has been applied in various situations and has become a rule of thumb: the value of a small number of items in a group far outweighs that derived from the other items.

> Key Term
>
> **Pareto Principle** The generalization that, in any group of items, 80% of the value will be derived from 20% of the items. If a car owner's manual, for example, were to list 20 features, you can expect to derive 80% of your satisfaction from the purchase of that car from only four of those features. Many people use this principle to weigh the relative importance of activities in setting priorities.

How does this translate into real terms? Here are a few concrete and familiar examples of the Pareto Principle at work:

- 20% of the mail received yields 80% of the value obtained; the other 80% of the mail is virtually worthless.
- 80% of a company's sales come from 20% of its clients.
- 80% of your time on the phone is spent with only 20% of the people you call during the course of the year.
- Most people derive 80% of the value they receive from their computers from 20% of the computer's functions.
- 20% of a company's employees take 80% of its sick leave.
- 80% of the clothes you wear regularly are only 20% of what hangs in your closet.

The Pareto Principle offers a powerful tool for change. More value is derived from the time you spend targeting 20% of your clients than from the time you spend on the other 80%. Your telephone's speed-dial list should probably be updated to account for the 20% of people you actually call regularly. Those who read your reports will probably derive 80% of the value you put in them from 20% of the information.

Remember when your parents had days when they received no mail? Remember when people had only three or four TV channels? (If you're too young to remember this and can't believe it, ask your parents or grandparents.) Those were the days when the Pareto Principle touched only a few people's lives and in only limited ways. But now? Consider the following statistics:

- Americans receive 15 billion faxes yearly; that figure is expected to double every two to three years.
- 50,000 books are published yearly in the United States.
- The American reading public has about 11,000 magazines to choose from.
- The average cable television system carries over 100 channels and emerging technology could expand that to well over 500 choices.
- You'll probably spend eight months out of your life going through the mail.

It has become impossible to keep abreast of the stream of information that washes past us. To stay ahead, people must become selective. They must concentrate on that 20% of information that yields 80% of the value and reject the rest.

This principle can be so broadly applied that the examples are virtually unlimited. Keeping in mind that 80% of your value to your company almost certainly derives from 20% of your work product (and from 20% of the time you spend at work), you might consider searching for ways to improve that ratio. Real productivity—and the advancement that very often accompanies it—may well be a function of discovering how to make the most of the Pareto Principle.

Manager's Checklist for Chapter 3

- ❑ The A, B, C system is a practical and familiar way to prioritize your daily activities.
- ❑ Index cards, Post-it® notes, or magnetic boards can make the ABC system even more flexible.
- ❑ If you or your company are driven by results, the inventory system is an attractive option.
- ❑ Treating time in terms of monetary-like payoffs frequently brings measurable precision to your prioritizing.
- ❑ The 80/20 formula, or Pareto Principle, often affords unexpected and fascinating insights to buttress priorities.

Procrastination: The Thief of Time

Everyone does it. Everyone feels guilty when they do it. And everyone resolves never to do it again. But they do. Everyone procrastinates. Procrastination—the cat burglar of time management—steals into your life and whisks away one of the most valuable assets you possess.

Of course, not everyone regrets putting things off. Indeed, some people—having decided that it's so ingrained in human nature that there's no use struggling against it—take pride in their status as procrastinators. There's even a National Procrastinators Club. Really. You can find out all about it at www.procrastinators.org. It has about 10,000 members—no one is really sure, though, since the full list has never been compiled or completed. The group occasionally tries to have meetings, but customarily postpones them. The same person was president for decades because the club never got around to holding new elections. And dues ... well, collecting them must be an interesting process.

What's Behind Procrastination?

Procrastination can be a thoroughly amusing concept, indeed. But, as with all things humorous, there are some underlying deep and darker forces. At the root of procrastination, argue psychologists, almost always lurks some hidden fear or conflict that urges us to put things off. A person may be obliged to achieve certain results, but a multitude of opposing emotions serve to short-circuit action. Although the procrastinator may act as if the threat, fear, or conflict is gone, it's still there—both in the real world and in the person's subconscious—where it generates stress and, ultimately, corrodes success.

Time management experts have identified the eight most typical causes of procrastination, shown in Figure 4-1.

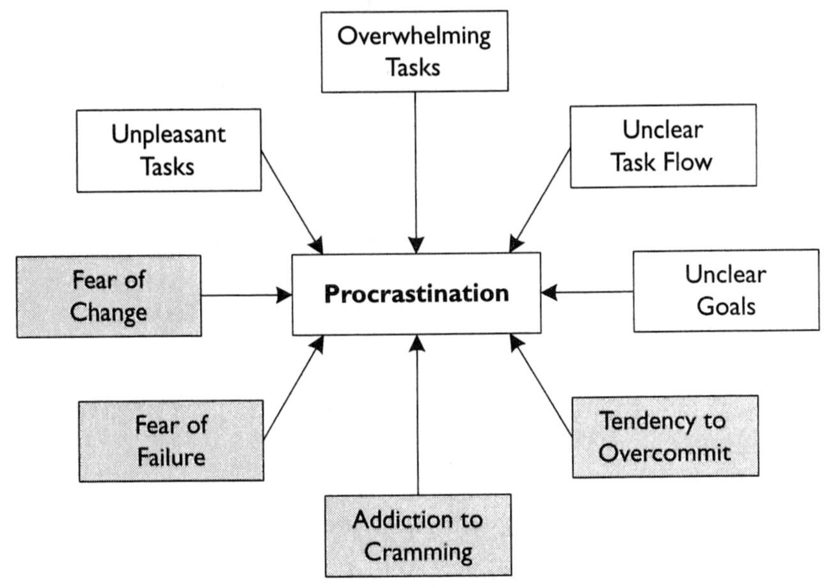

Figure 4-1. Causes of procrastination

Internal Forces

Note that four of the causes (those in the shaded boxes) are primarily inner rooted. They arise, for the most part, from the procrastinator's psyche. When we have certain tendencies or per-

MISTAKE PROOFING

Combating Perfectionism

Three simple questions should help you decide whether your approach to a task is too "perfectionist":

1. Is the payoff worth the effort you're putting into it?
2. Is there actually a simpler, less time-consuming way to do it?
3. Are you neglecting other projects in order to make this project "perfect"?

If the answer to any of these questions is yes, you're probably exerting more effort than the project either requires or deserves.

sonality traits, they can manifest themselves in very different situations. If, for example, you tend to fear failure and you procrastinate largely for that reason, you'll procrastinate on any task at which you might fear that you'll fail.

If you answer yes to any of the following questions, you may have the tendency to procrastinate embedded in your personality:

- While in school, did you usually cram before a test?
- Do you often put off returning a call to someone you don't like, even if it's important?
- Do you wait until you have dental problems to see your dentist?
- Have you had an unintentional late finance charge in the last three months?
- Do you wait until a deadline looms before beginning important projects?

To defeat procrastination you need to put considerable energy into behavior change. Sound impossible? It's not. A number of proven and clear strategies can enable you to effect genuine and lasting change.

External Forces

Even if you usually don't procrastinate, your environment can impose procrastination on you. Figure 4-1 gives, in the clear unshaded boxes, the four typical external reasons for procrastination. This is not to say that psychological reasons aren't involved. There must be some. But unpleasant or overwhelming tasks—and unclear goals or task flow—are enough to make anyone want to postpone the inevitable.

Fighting the Forces

Internal causes for procrastination are more difficult to attack than external ones, but once psychological obstacles are conquered, they're conquered for all tasks. If you procrastinate because of a fear of change, that fear will color many different kinds of tasks. Once you conquer this fear, you'll be able to approach most tasks with renewed energy.

While a single internal cause can make you procrastinate on many tasks, external causes for procrastination tend to be task-specific. So, if you're putting off doing something for an external cause, you can cope with that cause and stop procrastinating—but that victory probably won't help you with other external causes that are making you procrastinate on other tasks.

Why Do You Procrastinate?

Examine Figure 4-1 carefully. Is it easy for you to identify the category that is least relevant to your own procrastination tendencies? Can you easily identify the one that you feel is the principal cause of your own delaying tactics?

If it's easy to discern which typical causes of procrastination are the most and least relevant to your behavior, then you're probably well clear of a procrastination rut—or, if you are in a rut, the challenge of getting out may be relatively simple for you. If, however, you found it somewhat difficult to identify the least and most relevant causes, your procrastination may be caused by a complex web of interdependent factors. You face an uphill battle. You'll have to be tenacious. But you can win.

If you identified the factor most relevant to your procrastination as internal (psychological) and the factor least relevant as external, then you'll need to look deeply into yourself for the answers. On the other hand, if the factors most influencing your procrastination are external, you'll have to do all you can to reshape the environment you work and live in.

What Are You Procrastinating About?

So far, this discussion has been about general categories. It's now time to get specific. What are you putting off right now?

Make a list of business duties, personal responsibilities, and long-term goals that you've done nothing about (e.g., changing careers, getting married), short-term tasks (that complaint letter), telephone calls, a vacation—anything you can think of, large or small, that you should be doing but haven't gotten around to.

You may be surprised at the number of tasks backlogged in your mind. Out of sight, out of mind, right? One common subconscious method of procrastination involves simply putting certain chores or tasks out of your mind. Your first step in controlling your urge to procrastinate, then, is pushing these items back to the forefront of your consciousness, where they belong.

The Eight Factors

For each item on your list, try to identify which of the eight procrastination causes from Figure 4-1 probably reflects the major reason you're putting off this task. This will give you clues as to what must be cast off before you can take action. Some of the tasks may have more than one reason causing you to procrastinate.

There are proven strategies that will allow you to surmount the barriers—and perhaps get you started on the very things you've been neglecting.

1. The task seems unpleasant. Is this your single most important reason for not completing the tasks on your list? If so, you're typical. This is, by far, the most commonly given reason for procrastination. After all, what could be easier to put off than reprimanding an employee, washing the dishes, preparing a speech, or making a dental appointment?

Five strategies can help you take on a task that you avoid because it's unpleasant:

TRICKS OF THE TRADE

Delegating

Chapter 6 will consider delegation in more detail, but it's a good idea to start thinking about it now. In your personal life, for instance, many opportunities exist for you to delegate tasks that you tend to procrastinate on. For example, many services will pick up and deliver products for you: pharmacies, dry cleaners, even grocery and office supply stores. These services can save you time on a chore you might find unpleasant. If you've been in charge of writing checks to pay the family bills, you can arrange to have many of these bills paid automatically by your bank. Or perhaps your spouse would be willing to take on this task for you. If you tend to put it off, it might very well be a candidate for delegation.

- *Do it the first thing in the day.* Often, if you can do an unpleasant task before you've had much time to think about it, it will seem easier. Or, if you do want to spend some time thinking, why not think about how unburdened you'll feel for the rest of the day when the task is done?
- *The night before, place the task where you can't miss it.* Put that complaint letter you must respond to in the middle of your desk. When you walk into your office, it will be hard to avoid.
- *Find somebody else to do it.* Remember this: what you find unpleasant, someone else might actually enjoy.
- *Make an advantage/disadvantage list.* This is for heavy-duty kinds of unpleasant tasks. List all the positive things that will result from getting the task done and then list all the disadvantages to doing it. Just seeing it all on paper may relieve your anxiety.
- *Use the "measles" approach.* Several time management

Smart Managing

Eating the Elephant

Question: "How do you eat an elephant?" Answer: "One bite at a time."

There's great wisdom in this venerable saying. Overwhelming responsibilities or projects that seem indigestible—the very kind we often dangerously procrastinate on—become easier to deal with when we nibble away at them one bite at a time.

For Example

Break It Down

Henry Ford, credited with designing the first production line, once maintained, "Nothing is particularly hard if you divide it into small jobs." Following his own advice, Ford examined the apparently huge task of assembling an automobile and broke it down into logical, sequential steps. What seems obvious to us now—the production line process—was, however, innovative in his time. Virtually any complex task is open to the same approach Ford took with the automobile.

experts counsel the following strategy: every time you handle a paper-based document you don't want to deal with, put a red dot on it. Once it starts looking like it has the measles, you'll get the message.

2. The task seems overwhelming. Herculean, massive, gargantuan, endless—all these terms can be used to describe that proposal you have to write, that meeting you must plan, or that home remodeling project you should undertake. The task is not necessarily unpleasant; in fact, you may even look forward to accomplishing it. But it's so huge and overwhelming that you just don't know where to start. A common example of feeling overwhelmed is writer's block, paralysis by the enormity of a writing project.

Here are three strategies to help you get a handle on the project:

- *Divide and conquer.* Breaking a major job into small pieces can help conquer an overwhelming task. Chapter 5 discusses this strategy in detail.
- *Find a solitary place to do it.* Is there a room at work or at home where few people ever go? Hide yourself there to do the task that shouldn't be interrupted. Close your office door and make clear to everyone that you are not to be disturbed. Or go off on a "work vacation" to do what you must in pleasant surroundings, undisturbed.
- *Ride the momentum.* Once you get going, keep going as long as your concentration stays strong and fresh. But when your mind wanders, stop. Take a break.

3. The task flow is unclear or unplanned. Disorganized plans are common grounds for procrastination. One useful approach to attacking the problem of task flow comes from a process control system called TQM.

The TQM Solution

In the late 1940s, W. Edwards Deming, a statistical control analyst, devised a process control system that came to be known as Total Quality Management (TQM). He tried to convince several U.S. companies to apply it to their assembly lines, but no one seemed interested. Undaunted, Deming went to Japan, where business leaders rapidly adopted his theories.

Many people feel that Japan's subsequent economic success was attributable in large measure to Deming's system. The truth is far more complex. Japan's cultural values had a great

Total Quality Management (TQM) A process control system devised by W. Edwards Deming. In his book, *Out of the Crisis* (1982), Deming set out 14 points as essential. Although devised for manufacturing, they are easily adapted to all business situations.

1. Create constancy of purpose by investing in the future.
2. Quality must become a philosophy of total dedication.
3. Don't inspect bad quality out; build quality in from the start.
4. Don't award business on price alone.
5. Improve constantly on production and service.
6. Institute training.
7. Institute leadership.
8. Drive out fear.
9. Break down staff barriers.
10. Eschew slogans or targets.
11. Eliminate numerical quotas.
12. Encourage pride of workmanship.
13. Promote education and self-improvement.
14. Transform the company from the top down, involving everyone.

It is worth noting that the current management emphasis on the concept of "Six Sigma" is basically the disciplined systemization of many of the concepts of TQM.

deal to do with its economic success—and with the ways in which Deming's system was implemented. Still, TQM has much to offer. Indeed, the U.S. military and several American companies, seeking to compete with Asian entrepreneurs, made a virtual religion of it.

Though TQM has fallen somewhat out of favor, certain processes it popularized are still quite worthwhile. Of all the TQM procedures, none is more relevant to time management than flowcharting. TQM proponents tackle each project by visualizing its flow. Absolutely every step is plotted, often using the symbols or icons in Figure 4-2.

> Key Term
> **Flowchart** A diagram that displays the step-by-step progression through a procedure or system, frequently using lines connecting the steps to indicate direction or flow.

Figure 4-3 shows an example of an abridged flowchart.

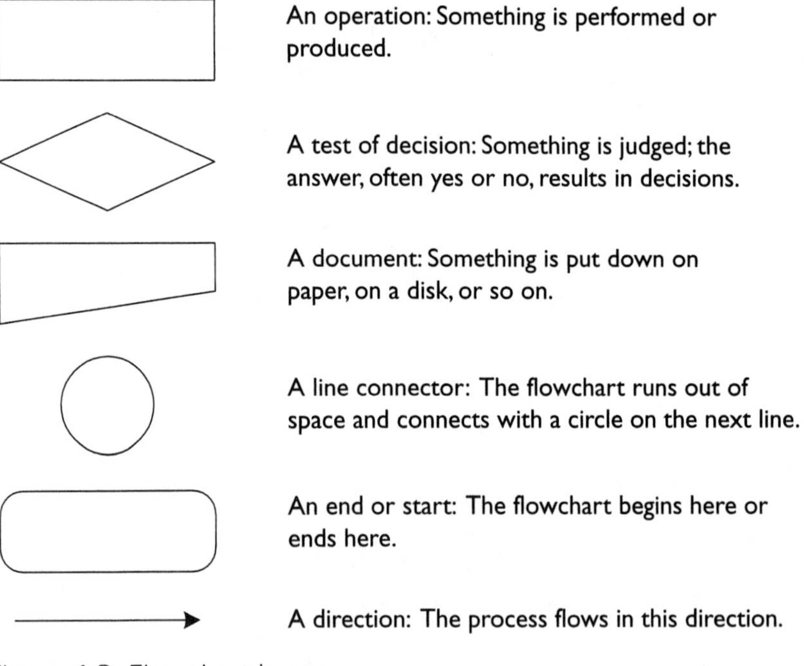

Figure 4-2. Flowchart icons

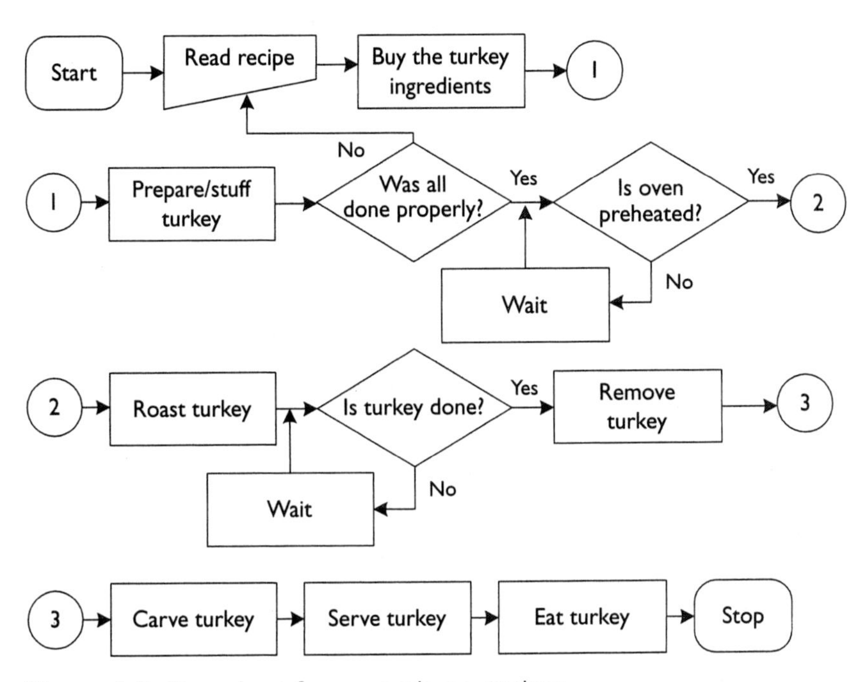

Figure 4-3. Flowchart for preparing a turkey

Examine the flowchart in Figure 4-3. Were any steps left out? If so, where would you insert them?

You might try to apply this method to some of the items you listed earlier as awaiting action. Above all, remember that flowcharting often leads to significant savings of time that might otherwise have been spent later trying to rein in the details of a hazy or stubbornly complicated project.

4. Your goals are unclear. When you set a goal, be precise. "Reorganize my office space" may be insufficiently clear. How would you like your office space to be organized? What specific needs are dictating your desire to reorganize? Are items you need daily stored in inaccessible places? Are non-current items taking up too much room? Do you need a better light source? Make general goals into specific goals by reminding yourself what it is, specifically, that makes the goal a goal.

In certain situations—especially in business—goals should be not only clear but also measurable. Saying, "Our sales will

CAUTION!

Waiting for Other People

There's one other external factor that might lead to procrastination: waiting for other people. You may be an angel of timely behavior, but your boss, your spouse, or your employee may not be. Changing someone else's behavior is even more difficult than changing your own. Here are a few ideas that may help:

- Set precise timelines and deadlines for others.
- Set false, early deadlines, to make it more probable that they'll actually finish on time.
- Communicate your frustration with their behavior, if necessary.
- Encourage them to use some of the strategies outlined in this chapter to overcome their tendency to procrastinate.

increase significantly" is less productive and has less impact than saying, "Our goal is to increase sales by 12%."

5. You fear change. This is one of the more deeply psychological reasons for procrastination. All living things are creatures of habit. Doing something the way you've always done it seems safe. Making changes sometimes courts the unexpected—and the unexpected can sometimes be unpleasant. So fear of change is a natural, human reaction. But it can also be debilitating, encouraging procrastination and deferring changes that are useful and beneficial.

If you procrastinate because you're in a rut—because you're resisting change—any of the following might work for you:

- *Change your physical environment.* Old habits cling to old places. Try a new room, a new chair, a new office, a new anything. You'll be surprised how such a change can spark actions on duties you're avoiding.
- *Change your routines and patterns.* Take a different route to get to work. You may be surprised at how you might feel toward a procrastinated obligation when you get to the office.
- *Do nothing.* Just walk into your home or office, sit down, and stare at the wall. You'll soon be so bored that a change will be precisely what you want.

6. You fear failure. The most confident people fear failing at something, so they put it off, sometimes forever. A good example is public speaking. People fear making a mistake in front of a large group of people because they believe that their failure will be magnified. In most surveys, the fear of a failed speech ranks higher than the fear of death.

Truman Capote once said, "Failure is the condiment that gives success its flavor." Franklin D. Roosevelt put it more famously: "The only thing we have to fear is fear itself."

7. You tend to overcommit. Many people are so dedicated, ambitious, or enthusiastic that they take on far more than they should—at work, at home, or in their communities. Different factors may drive this tendency—the inability to say no, a desire to please, or even merely the otherwise great virtues of a zest for life and a broad range of interests.

But no one can do it all—certainly not all at the same time. If, in looking over the list of pending tasks you composed earlier in this chapter, you find one or two items you could (and should) unburden yourself of, it's possible that you tend to take on too much. In the future, before volunteering to take on new commitments, take a few moments to review those commitments you've already made but haven't completed. You may wish to engage in a very useful form of procrastination—putting off new commitments until you complete the ones still pending.

8. You're addicted to cramming. For some people, doing something at the last minute triggers a rush of adrenaline that fuels them on. This is a dangerous habit because:

- Last-minute work increases the odds of making a mistake.
- You have no time to correct mistakes—or sometimes even to discover them.
- A new, unexpected demand may come up that will steal time from your last-minute sprint and hurt the quality of both tasks.

Five Minutes

What can you accomplish in five minutes? Sometimes, important things:

- Return an e-mail.
- Make an appointment.
- Leave a voicemail message.
- Write a page of text.
- Create an agenda for a meeting.
- Research a point.
- Write a thank-you note.
- Locate a missing source.
- Ask a colleague a question you need the answer to.
- Read a short message.
- Clarify something you were unclear about.

Often, if you can promise yourself to devote the next five minutes to a task, you'll find that it stretches into 10 or 15 minutes and you accomplish more than you thought you might when you began.

It's hard to overcome cramming. You must convince yourself that cramming is dangerous. And you must try all of the strategies mentioned earlier—flowcharting, the measles approach, dividing and conquering, and so on—to aid you in your efforts.

Conclusion

One final thought. Procrastination can be profitable—for others. Federal Express, fax machines, belated greeting cards, and extended preholiday store hours are all examples of products or services that make some of their money from procrastinators. So, if procrastination is so common that businesses depend on it for profit, it's almost certain that you—if you're not abnormal—tend to procrastinate in some situations, at least. If you can learn to control this very common tendency, you'll have taken a very large step toward using your time more effectively.

CAUTION!

Putting off the Inevitable

One way to create personal motivation to begin a task you're procrastinating on is to promise yourself a reward at its conclusion. Another way is to acknowledge the negative consequences of procrastination. When tempted to procrastinate, ask yourself, am I willing to suffer the consequences of ...

- Missing this deadline?
- Having no time to check for mistakes?
- Producing inferior work?
- The stress associated with the resulting time pressures?

Manager's Checklist for Chapter 4

❑ There are both internal and external factors that influence the tendency to procrastinate.

❑ Hidden fears and conflicts lie at the root of most procrastination. These can be conquered.

❑ Flowcharts can help you organize and focus on a complex task.

❑ Other people's behavior is often harder to change than your own, but if you work at it vigorously, you can encourage the transformation of their behavior.

Rocks, Blocks, Goals, and Clusters

One day a time management expert spoke to a group of business students. He set a wide-mouthed, one-gallon mason jar on the table in front of him. Then he produced about a dozen fist-sized rocks and placed them carefully, one at a time, inside the jar.

When the jar was filled to the top and no more rocks would fit inside, he asked, "Is the jar full?" Everyone in the class answered, "Yes."

Then he asked, "Really?" He reached under the table and pulled out a bucket of gravel. Then he dumped some gravel in and shook the jar, causing pieces of gravel to work down into the spaces among the big rocks. He asked the group once more, "Is the jar full now?" By this time the class was on to him. "Probably not," one of them answered.

"Good!" he exclaimed. He reached under the table and brought out a bucket of sand. He started adding sand to

the jar and it slid into the spaces remaining among the rocks and gravel. Once more he asked the question, "Is this jar full?" "No!" the class shouted.

"Good," he shouted back, grabbing a pitcher of water and pouring it into the jar until it was full to the brim.

Then he looked up at the class and asked, "What's the point of what I just did?"

One student raised her hand and replied, "The point is, no matter how full your schedule seems to be, if you try really hard, you can always fit some more things into it."

"No!" the speaker replied. "That's not the point. The truth this illustration teaches us is, if you don't put the big rocks in first, you'll never get them all in."

There's only one way to get all of the rocks, gravel, sand, and water of our lives into the jar that is time—intelligent scheduling. We have to be able to identify which of our activities are rocks and which are gravel, sand, and water.

The number of things we do and the order in which we do them should be determined by the size of the jar. You can't get everything in if you don't consider the big things first. Every line in your organizer need not be completely filled with minutiae. But you do need to take priorities into account when scheduling and consecrate blocks of your time for tasks that *must* fit into your day. This chapter will discuss things that deserve those sacred segments of your time.

Establishing Goals

Ask some truly successful people what accounts for their achievements and you'll often hear this answer: goals. Indeed, clear goals are the fulcrum on which all prioritizing turns. To set goals is worth a good block of your time. Without goals your time will be aimless.

But what kinds of goals? What must goals be?

- **Attainable.** Successful people set goals that are ambitious

I Don't Have Time!

Have you ever thought to yourself, "But I don't have *time* to set goals! I'm too busy working!"

It's probably true that taking the time to set goals now will cut into the time you've reserved for other activities. But in the long run, it's one of the most effective time-saving strategies you can pursue.

It simply isn't possible to maximize the use of your time if you don't have a clear idea of what you're trying to accomplish—both short term and long term. Carving out a small amount of time each week to devote to reviewing your goals can work wonders for providing the focus you need to allocate your time productively.

yet realistic. Cycles of success mark achievers' lives. When such people fail, it isn't from a lack of planning or effort. Dreamers, on the other hand, set unreachable goals. They ride a rollercoaster of ups and downs, sometimes never making it to the top of the first hill.

- **Measurable.** Imagine a football game with no yard lines, end zones, goal posts, scoreboard, clock, or even clear-cut teams—just a bunch of players whose goal is to pass a football, run around, and collide. It might be fun to watch for a while, but not for long. The chaos would soon drive the fans out of the stadium. Shortly thereafter, the players, unmotivated and confused, would wander off the field.

  To work without clear-cut, *measurable* goals is, in

TRICKS OF THE TRADE

Measuring Your Goals

"Measuring" implies "quantifying." But some or most of your goals are somewhat abstract, like "spend quality time with my family" or "prepare presentation for the Acme project." How can you "measure"—or "quantify"—such amorphous goals?

Easy. Translate them into numbers. Most of the things we do in life can be thought of in terms of time or money or both. You can usually place a dollar value or a time value on any goal. For example, getting specific on how *much* quality time you want to spend with your family will allow you to measure your success. Setting the dollar amount that you want the Acme project to realize will help you to assess, in retrospect, how well you prepared that presentation.

reality, not much more productive or engaging than our imaginary football game. To motivate yourself and others—to know if you have won—you absolutely need goals that can be measured.

- **Written.** "I read it, so it must be true!" Something written has a peculiar power to convince. Writing down your objectives and having others read them (if you supervise them, they may need to read your goals) brings authority, accountability, and permanence to your priorities. The Sheraton Anchorage has printed goal statements all over its service corridors; it's one of the best-run hotels in the country.
- **Accountable.** Without accountability, goals melt away, forgotten. Remain flexible; feedback may prompt you to revise targets you set for yourself or for others. But hold to your goals.
- **Deadlined.** If you set a deadline for your tasks, you'll have a much better chance of achieving your goal. Better yet, tell someone else that you set that deadline. It will make you more accountable.

The same applies to deadlines you set for others. Always give a precise time of completion and periodically review progress toward your objectives.

Goals, of course, can be long- or short-term. But for some reason, we often fail to set aside blocks of time for serious long-term goal setting. Each year—perhaps as a New Year's resolu-

For Example

Describing Your Goals

30 years ago, a certain woman set as her goal "to have a body like Elizabeth Taylor's." How likely would it be today that she'd set *exactly the same goal in exactly the same words?* Bodies change over time, fashions change over time, and the goal today would almost certainly be expressed differently.

It's important that you say what you mean when setting goals—and that you review your words from time to time to determine whether or not they continue to express what you really want to achieve.

tion—you should make a list of at least three personal and three professional long-term goals, indicating how each will be measured and a deadline for achievement. Prioritize these goals, deciding which is your A goal, your B goal, and your C goal. Then put this list in a prominent place—someplace where its presence will motivate you to continued action.

Leave Me Alone!

Usually, both workplace and home are environments of near-constant interaction. An employee requires clearer direction for an upcoming meeting. Kids need help with homework. The phone rings. The doorbell rings. A fax spews out something that demands action. The dog barks. It's one thing after another.

Yet certain responsibilities require solitude. Interruptions are like so many logs on a railroad track. Each creates big bumps in the ride; one might derail the whole train. To detour around this problem, consider the following:

- Identify a time each week when you're least likely to have vital interactions. Block off that time (at least two hours) on your calendar or weekly organizer for uninterrupted work. You need not even know what you'll do during that period: there will always be something. (If not, though, you can always work on those D priorities.)
- If you're at work, make sure that everyone knows about

TRICKS OF THE TRADE

Public and Private Time

Time management expert Stephanie Winston suggests dividing your time according to activities that you designate either as "private" or "public." *Public* activities might include anything in which others are involved—either scheduled meetings or unanticipated intrusions. *Private* activities include such items as paperwork, correspondence, reading, research, and planning. Then, she suggests, create blocks of time that are devoted to either public or private tasks.

It's a good idea, as well, to alternate public and private time. That way, those who want to meet with you will know that they don't have long to wait before you'll be available to them.

your "sacred" hours. The same, if you can pull it off (and need to), might even be practical at home.

- Hang a "do not disturb" sign on your door. Keep the door closed. (If you have a work cubicle and not an enclosed office, tape the sign in a strategic spot.) Divert calls to voicemail. Doing this, of course, requires some tact, but if you're productive, your peers should respect your quiet times as a mark of dedication and efficiency, not aloofness or indolence.
- Find a "secret" place to work. Often, there's some conference room, function hall, or other space in your building where you could go and work, uninterrupted and undiscovered. When you feel the need to work undisturbed, go there. It might even be someplace unexpected, like the local library or a seldom-used corner of a nearby hotel's lobby. (This strategy works for some home responsibilities, too.)
- Come to work very early or stay late. This, of course, has something to do with your body rhythms (discussed later in this chapter), as well as the patterns of your fellow workers and of family members. Also, some businesses don't encourage flextime (the ability to work your own schedule). They still expect you to work until 6 p.m., even if you came in at 7 a.m. However, the times when others aren't in the office and callers don't expect you to be there can be the most productive of all.
- Have lunch when no one else does. If your stomach can accept it and your schedule permits it, eating lunch at 11 a.m. or 2 p.m. will carve out

Make an Appointment TRICKS OF THE TRADE

When you have an important project due and it's hard to find time to work on it, make an appointment with yourself. Write it in your calendar and—when the time comes—treat the job with the same respect you'd give to an appointment with another person. Close your office door, let voicemail take your calls, and devote your attention to the task at hand.

that 12-to-2 block of time for what can be a relatively quiet period in the office.

Doing Nothing

Up to now, this chapter has examined ways to concentrate blocks of time for serious work. But what about time for taking it easy, socializing, just doing nothing? Is that productive?

It can be. Working past your optimum level of energy and attention can be self-defeating; you could be spinning your wheels and going nowhere. Pausing to relax and recuperate can reenergize your work and make you more productive. It can also make work seem less like work. And if you drive your employees to squeeze effort out of every minute, you'll be left with people who are unmotivated, burned out, or seemingly happy workaholics. Is this what you want?

Another reason for carving out totally unplanned times in your schedule: it allows you leeway to deal with the unexpected. An anecdote about Henry Kissinger comes to mind. The well-known statesman is said to have remarked to a reporter, "Next week there can't be any crisis. My schedule is already full."

A recent study discovered an interesting fact: executives who did not fill in every single time block in their calendars, who left broad stretches of blank space, were actually more productive and less stressed than their overscheduled colleagues. Your day need not be seamless. Give your schedule room to breathe.

Clustering

A term that is in frequent use in time management, *clustering*, refers to the practice of assembling tasks. Clustering—for many reasons—makes activity far more fruitful, efficient, and compact.

One example: paying bills. Should you deal with them daily, as they come in, or pay them off in groups, perhaps once a week, when you're free to do so? The latter course of action generally works far better; you need to get the checkbook and stamps out only once, for example. More important, you're not letting the semi-chaotic flow of incoming bills dictate your behavior.

Clustering works especially well with outgoing phone calls. You assemble your list of phone calls to make the night before, then make them all during one block of time, preferably when the people you're calling are likely to be in and not barraged with calls from others.

> Key Term
>
> **Clustering** The activity of organizing and assembling a group of tasks that have something in common. For example, tasks might be grouped together because they're all small, requiring little time and/or effort. Gathering together documents that need to be photocopied and copying them all at the same time is an example of clustering. So is returning all phone calls during the same hour or researching several topics at the same time.

Clustering also works in reverse. Phone calls, for example, tend to stream in most heavily at certain times during the day. You should be prepared to receive them and to shape the rest of your daily schedule accordingly. Typically, the blocks of time between 10 and 11 a.m. and between 2 and 3 p.m. see the greatest amount of business telephone activity. Pareto analysis indicates that 80% of all calls generally come during 20% of the

> CAUTION!
>
> **Leak-Proof Clustering**
>
> Personal productivity coach David Allen warns that lists work only when they're "leak-proof." For example, if you cluster all of the documents you need to take to the copier but overlook one, you've totally defeated the purpose of clustering. That single extra trip to the copy machine can render the entire strategy ineffective.
>
> So when attempting to cluster your phone calls, for instance, try to be certain you're listing *everyone* you need to call. The more complete your list—the more comprehensive the collection of items you're clustering—the more effective the strategy will be. You might also consider asking your assistant, if you have one, to hold your calls during certain times, promising to have you return them at a more convenient time.

workday. If you're employed at a company that communicates across the country or around the world, of course, the pattern will be far more complex.

A useful exercise would be for you to chart the times of incoming calls for a week and attempt to identify patterns. If such patterns emerge, rethink the way you schedule your hours. Might there be a more efficient way to free up time for these calls (and minimize interruptions of tasks requiring intense concentration)? You might also repeat this exercise at different times of the year. For some businesses, phone work fluctuates dramatically according to month, season, or special event.

Discovering Patterns

Telephone patterns aren't the only ones worthy of attention. Many subtle and significant patterns lurk beneath the ebb and flow of business. Dedicating blocks of time to analyze patterns can yield powerful insights into the ways behavior can be managed. You may not be able to control the patterns that are set by others, but you can recognize those patterns and adapt your schedule accordingly. If you know that you're more likely to get visitors in the morning than in the afternoon, you can schedule activities that require long stretches of uninterrupted time when you're most likely to be left alone.

Do you know, for example, when most of your faxes come in? At what time the Federal Express delivery person usually arrives? When most e-mail is exchanged? When customers or suppliers are least likely to come

> Smart Managing
>
> **The 50% Rule**
>
> Whenever you schedule a meeting, add 50% to the time you schedule. One of the most schedule-wrecking problems most people face is the tendency to *underestimate* the time it will take to meet face-to-face with someone. Meetings can be unpredictable and events can sometimes wrench the timing out of your control. So just to be safe, plan for any meeting to take 50% longer than you think it needs to take. If the meeting ends early, you'll have that extra time available for a task you might not otherwise have had time to do.

to you? The better you're able to predict with some certainty normal events in your day, the easier it will be to adjust your scheduling to accommodate them.

What's Your Clock?

A morning person wakes and says, "Rise and shine! Up and at 'em!"

The night person responds, "Shut up and drop dead."

Each person marches through the day to the tick of a different clock. There's even a science that examines this phenomenon: *chronobiology*.

Some of our biological processes cue our energy and attention levels. For this reason, chronobiology has cultural implications for time management in general and prioritizing in particular. It provides important clues about how we should carve out our day.

Key Term

Chronobiology The science that studies how the body's systems relate to time. Brain chemistry, enzyme production, blood-sugar levels, hunger and satiation, sleep patterns, and even such arcane physical reactions to time as jet lag are all subjects of chronobiological study.

"Morning people" tend to wake easily and fully alert. They have a noticeable drop in energy in the early afternoon. "Mid-day people" are the most suited to the 9-5 schedule common at most companies, waking most usually between 7 and 8 a.m. Their energy tends to peak in the early afternoon and they most likely eat dinner around 7 p.m. "Evening people" sleep late and tend to wake groggy. They aren't bothered by early morning light—they can sleep through almost anything in the morning. They're often awake long after others are snug in bed and are the prime audience for late-night talk shows and vintage movies.

Is it easy to determine whether you're a morning, mid-day, or evening person? Not entirely. Energy can wax and wane in minicycles throughout the day. So try tracking for a week those times at which you feel most alert and energetic, those when—

though still alert—you'd like to take a break, and those when you feel you really *need* a break. Then take advantage of the patterns you find by scheduling your activities according to the following recommendations, whenever possible:

When you're *fully alert*, schedule:

- Large, involved projects
- Critical, pressing matters
- Important reading
- Material that's potentially boring
- Meeting with your boss
- Meetings and phone calls where you mostly listen
- Anything that requires you to be more passive than active
- Anything that should not be interrupted

When you're *alert*, schedule:

- Mathematically based activities (e.g., preparing a financial report)
- Meetings with colleagues or those you supervise
- Dining
- Moderately interesting reading
- Creative work
- Physical activity that requires concentration (e.g., driving)
- Anything that would not suffer from brief, important interruptions
- Most writing, typing, computer work

When you're *sluggish*, schedule:

- Short-duration projects
- A variety of brief tasks
- Activity that requires physical movement where concentration is not critical (e.g., walking to another floor or out to a store)
- Calls or meetings with people you like
- Interactive computer programs (e.g., a CD-ROM for training.)
- Things you find extremely interesting

A Few Hints

When you feel sluggish, you can write and do computer work if you're composing something interesting. But beware: you're likely to make more mistakes and to become mentally saturated after a brief time. Variety is the key. Movement and innately interesting activity work well, since they jolt you out of indifference. Once out of your lethargy, you'll be able to handle activities usually reserved for alert states.

When you're in an energy trough, avoid meetings or calls where your role is passive. They can be deadly to you. If you have no choice, force yourself to participate and certainly take notes. Such actions will help keep you sharp.

Avoid doing any one thing for longer than an hour and a half. Alertness seems to fluctuate in 90-minute cycles. Beyond 90 minutes, alertness plummets.

Body rhythms seem genetically determined, but they can be reprogrammed somewhat. Heavy food and carbohydrates (sugars, especially) will plunge most people into sluggishness. Coffee and soft drinks (health concerns aside) will briefly increase alertness. A meal of lean protein energizes most people for hours. A nap (a luxury rarely affordable in our culture) can snap a person out of the doldrums. Usually 30 to 40 minutes is enough.

Crossing time zones wreaks havoc on internal body clocks. It takes about one day per time zone crossed to fully readjust. In the meantime, your body will try to honor both time zones. (A good trick is to get plenty of outdoor light in the afternoon and early evening. The body takes its temporal clues from sunlight.)

Physical performance peaks in the afternoon and early evening. If you need to remember something for a very long time, study it in the afternoon. Mornings favor short-term memory. Your senses become sharpest in the late afternoon and early evening. Mid-afternoon is the best time to do uncomplicated or repetitive chores.

Conclusion

Blocking off your time for goal setting, scheduling uninterrupted moments, clustering, and adjusting to patterns are not easy. But when you practice these strategies, they can help you take control of your life. Yet all the time blocks in the world cannot enable you to do everything there is to do. Sometimes somebody else has to do it. Chapter 6 discusses this topic.

Manager's Checklist for Chapter 5

- ❑ Carving up responsibilities often makes them far easier to deal with.
- ❑ Goal setting is indispensable to achievement.
- ❑ Goals should be attainable, measurable, written, accountable, and deadlined.
- ❑ Uninterrupted time—either for work or for relaxation—can substantially enhance productivity.
- ❑ Detecting patterns of activity can lead to better prioritizing.
- ❑ Body rhythms have a profound effect on the way you conduct your daily activities. Adjust to them for maximum results.
- ❑ Although everyone is different, research points to several generalizations about most people's biological rhythms.

How to Delegate Effectively

"It's not my job."

That's a phrase fraught with implications. Whom do you imagine saying this—someone who will do nothing unless it's spelled out in a contract? That's one rather disheartening interpretation.

But this phrase has a potential second meaning. There may be a lot of tasks you're doing right now that are not your job, such as things you should delegate or things that should never have been delegated to you. Delegating isn't limited only to executives, managers, and others with "power." Even if you think you're in no position to delegate, this chapter still has insights for you.

To Whom Can You Delegate?

The obvious answer is: to those you manage and/or supervise. This is delegating *downward,* when you have full authority over the person to whom you're delegating. But keep this key con-

TRICKS OF THE TRADE

The Economics of Delegation

A critical rule about delegation is this: whenever possible, delegate tasks to the person who is paid the least yet has the necessary skills and training to perform the task.

Most often, when someone is paid to do a job that someone who earns less could do as well, money is wasted. The most economical—in every sense—use of an employee's time is in performing tasks that are at the high end of his or her ability and training.

This includes you. So when you fail to delegate a task others could do as efficiently, your own value to the company is diminished, as well as the value to the company of the person to whom you might have delegated it.

cept in mind: it succeeds only if you assign responsibilities to the right person. For convenience or because of a lack of choice, we're sometimes forced to delegate to someone inappropriate for the task. This may be the single greatest cause of failure. Inappropriate delegation can lead to unsatisfactory results or to employees who hide behind their job descriptions.

Targeting the right person for the job should be your main priority. And if there's no appropriate person, you may have to hire one.

Delegation isn't always downward. It can be *sideways* (*lateral*), too. That's the situation when you and the person to whom you're delegating are more or less equal in rank or level of authority.

Here are two examples of delegating laterally:

You write easily and well, but hate to talk on the phone. Meanwhile, a colleague hates writing but is a master of phone skills.

Consider swapping responsibilities, if there's enough flexibility in your organization to do so. You don't want to avoid developing necessary skills, of course, but it doesn't makes sense not to match tasks with aptitudes and interests if possible.

You have a client who will be coming to town to discuss a

Smart Managing

Outsourcing

Another form of delegating is *outsourcing*—hiring vendors for a fee to do certain jobs instead of assigning them to staff employees. Corporate downsizing has made outsourcing an increasingly powerful management tool. Many self-employed professionals offer their services, including such skills as clerical, computer programming, graphic design, and technical or management consulting. Often, firms will hire consultants to head a specific project or to create a new product.

Temporary and part-time workers are easy to locate through agencies that specialize in their services. If a time-consuming task will take valuable time to complete and will be worth less to your company than warranted by your salary, perhaps it's time to consider outsourcing the project.

> *contract. You find dealing with this individual very trying and time-consuming, because you find him overbearing and unfocused. However, one of your colleagues finds the client delightful.*
>
> Why not delegate the meeting to your colleague? You can always return the favor another time, perhaps when you're less pressed for time.

This section has identified two directions of delegation: downward and lateral. But there's a third, unexpected direction, as well: *upward* (see Figure 6-1 on the next page).

Sometimes someone above you assigns you a responsibility that shouldn't be yours. Other times, someone delegates to you so incompletely that you can't possibly perform the task competently.

Should you try to delegate the job back? Yes, if you do it very diplomatically. Here's the trick. Go to the person involved to seek "guidance." Express your enthusiasm about the project, but say that you feel you don't yet fully grasp the intent, procedures, or goals. Clarification might eliminate your need to delegate upward. Or your feedback may make the other person realize that he or she shouldn't have delegated this task, that he or she is the appropriate person to do it. You might even sug-

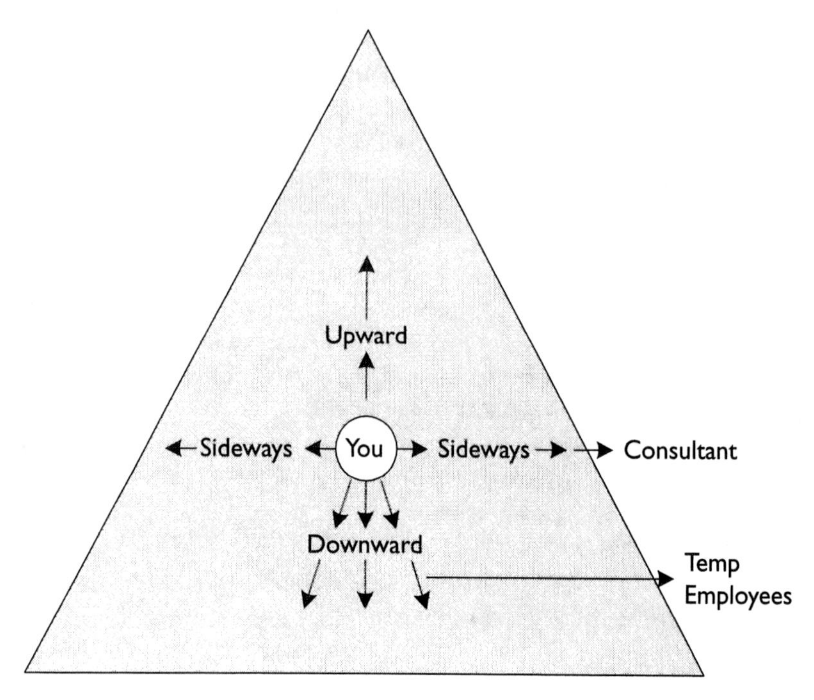

Figure 6-1. How can you delegate?

gest that a colleague would be better suited to the task (though you should clear it with your colleague first).

Delegating upward may be risky; then, again, boldness mixed with diplomacy can work wonders. Moreover, if the task is really outside your area of expertise, you'll be doing everyone (yourself included) a favor by finding a way to direct it toward someone better suited.

Delegating upward isn't always a matter of trying to "pass the buck" *back* to someone. Sometimes it's a matter of finding a way to pass it *forward* to someone better equipped to do it. If someone other than your boss asks you to do something you really don't have the authority to do, it's to everyone's benefit to suggest that your boss is probably better suited to the task. Delegating to your boss is sometimes the smartest thing you can do.

What Can You Delegate?

What types of tasks should you delegate? Two categories come to mind:

1. Tasks you don't want but that others might.
2. Tasks for which someone else might be better qualified.

A good place to begin exploring delegating possibilities is with a list of daily tasks—particularly routine ones—that might fit into either of the above categories. If you can find even one or two routine tasks that you might be able to delegate, you'll free up time to do those things you simply cannot delegate.

Why Is It Hard to Delegate?

Why is it so hard to delegate? One possible reason: dark, irrational thoughts may block the path. Here are six key reasons people give for not delegating a task. Ask yourself which ones most often apply to you.

Smart Managing

Don't Waste Your Time

Most tasks that cost more for you to do than for someone else are a waste of your time. Your value as an employee, manager, business owner, or officer consists in those special skills that you alone bring to your job.

So what kinds of tasks could you consider delegating or outsourcing, to maximize your value to the company? Some obvious examples:

- Database management
- Filing/clerical work
- Research
- Proofreading
- Telephone calls for simple information
- Making appointments
- Word processing
- Sales and marketing
- Computer programming

There are many other kinds of duties or tasks that you may find smart to delegate. Anything that can be done by someone who is paid less than you would be a prime task to delegate or outsource.

1. I'll lose control of the task.
2. I'm the only person who can do it right.
3. I'll look bad for giving it to someone else.
4. I'm afraid that I don't have the authority to delegate.
5. If the person to whom I delegate the task succeeds, I may become dispensable.
6. I just never thought of it.

CAUTION!

Let Go!

Most frequently, the reluctance to delegate is an expression of the need to *retain control.* As we pointed out earlier, attaining and holding control of situations is a necessary element of good time management, because it's impossible to make efficient use of time when you're at the mercy of people and situations outside your control.

However, if you insist on retaining control of *every detail* of the situations you're responsible for, you're failing to understand the real nature and benefits of control. An important measure of your influence may be how well you can exert your authority in a way that allows you to extend that authority. Unless you can relinquish control of little things, you have little hope of extending your command over the big things.

Sometimes, paradoxically, the only way to *take control* is to *relinquish control* over details that take up your precious time.

Once you've pinpointed the emotional barriers to delegating, you should feel freer to consider the possibility of assigning duties to others. Only in very rare instances are the above reasons for not delegating actually valid—and that's usually when you're the appropriate person for the job.

One final point: some people tend to *over*delegate. It's their way of shirking responsibility. That's poor motivation.

Another sin—to simply forget about a project once you assign it. *A reminder: delegate, don't abdicate.*

The Key Steps of Delegation

Deciding to delegate is a minor part of the battle. Doing it right is a much bigger challenge.

TOOLS

Communication Skills

When you need to delegate a task, good communication skills are vital—not only tact and sensitivity, but also the ability to specify exactly what you're asking the other person to do.

Here are some of the most common skills displayed by good communicators:

- They make eye contact.
- They treat people with respect.
- They listen as carefully as they speak.
- They organize their thoughts before they speak.
- They avoid using unnecessary jargon or technical terms.
- They don't assume.
- They encourage questions.
- They ask for feedback.
- They avoid speaking when they're angry.

Good communication skills are essential to effective delegation, because miscommunication can result in poor performance or resentment.

Delegating poorly leads almost invariably to disappointment, frustration, inefficiency, and, often, failure. Then, the manager may blame the person to whom he or she delegated the task, causing bad feelings, and not improve the way he or she delegates, so the delegation problems continue, in a downward spiral. Failure may also serve to reinforce all the delegation blocks listed earlier.

Here are 12 steps for masterful delegation:

1. Identify the task to be delegated. Once you've freed your mind from thoughts that defeat delegation, this step should become the easiest of all.

2. Trace out, on paper, the assigned project's flow. If the task is simple, this should be easy. If it's complicated, you may need to deploy a system similar to that described in Chapter 4. As an added help to you, the necessary steps of delegation are flowcharted in Figure 6-2.

If you assign work to a number of employees (either as part of a team project or each working on something different), be

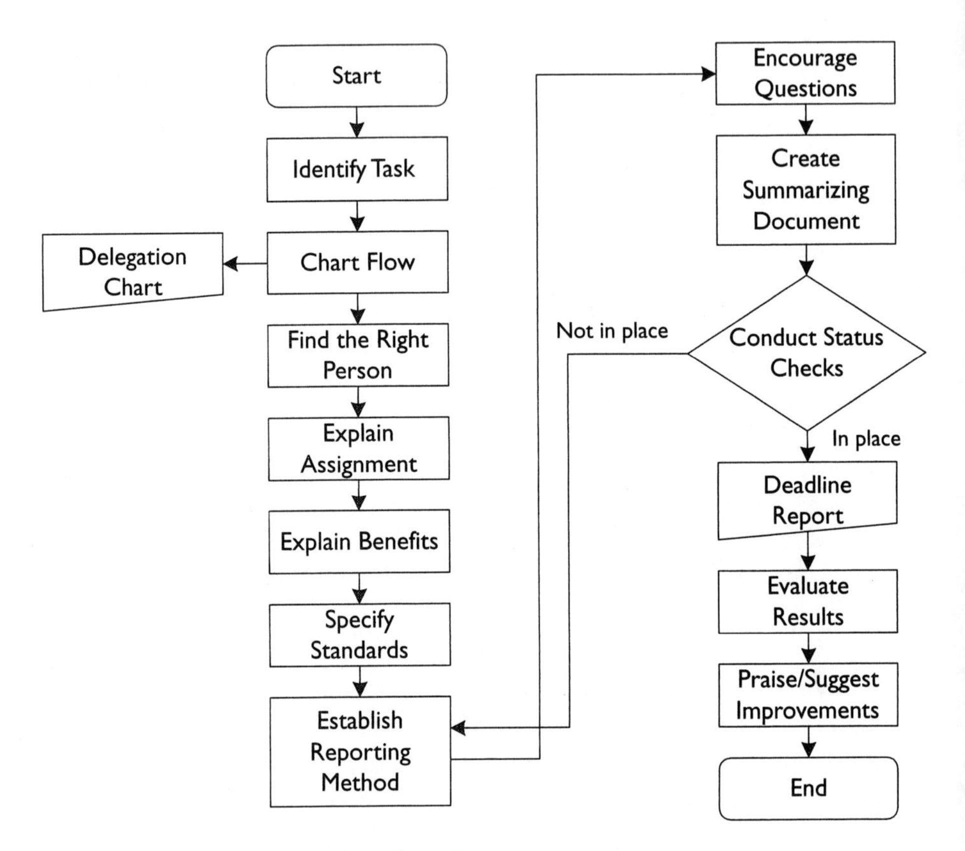

Figure 6-2. Delegation flowchart

sure to track your task assignments. Keep a record of the task delegated and the date you made the assignment, as well as dates for status review and task completion.

3. Find the right person. Once you've flowcharted the job, you should be in a better position to assign it to the right person. Be open-minded. Don't be constrained by existing roles. For example, the janitor might be just the right person to spearhead that new safety committee.

It's important to be aware of the unique talents and aptitudes of the people you work with and who work for you. Very often, people are capable of performing tasks—and would enjoy being asked to perform them—that no one has ever asked them to do. Those things that you know particular employees do well might serve as clues to those things that they've never done but for which they might have a hidden aptitude. The better you are at assessing the talents of those you manage—or of colleagues—the more successful you'll be at delegating.

4. Explain the assignment. Imagine trying to bake something with only half the recipe. You're virtually doomed to failure. And failure to lay out a careful and complete explanation of any task represents a sure recipe for disaster. Sit down with the person to whom you've delegated and walk through your flowchart's steps. Encourage questions. (A monologue rarely achieves clear communication.)

5. Explain the benefits. Everyone is concerned with the WIIFM—the What's in It for Me?—before buying something or buying *into* something. If you want to defuse resistance to the task you're delegating (and the it's-not-my-job syndrome), make liberal use of benefits language.

6. Specify your standards. Quality and accountability are two concepts that should guide all of your delegating. As when you create goals, you must convince the person to whom you delegate that you hold high expectations. Since you're sharing responsibility with him or her, you expect the best effort. Until his or her performance meets your standards, the task will remain incomplete.

> **Features and Benefits**
>
> MISTAKE PROOFING
>
> The following axiom is basic to almost all sales: don't sell the features, sell the benefits. It applies to delegation, too. Don't just outline the aspects of a task without giving reasons that motivate.
>
> Sure, maybe you have the authority to delegate the task, but selling it through the benefits to the person means that he or she is likely to consider it less an imposition and more an opportunity. And any smart manager knows the difference that makes in motivation and performance.

7. Discuss deadlines. Has anyone ever given you a job to do without a completion date? Did it somehow feel less important?

Deadlines help firm up prioritization. When you delegate, always set deadlines, including intermediary status review dates. Entertain input from the person you delegate to. If you empower the person in the process, by sharing responsibility from the start, you'll reinforce his or her motivation.

8. Establish a reporting method. To leave vague the reporting methods for intermediary and final deadlines is dangerous. Must feedback be written? Oral? Lengthy? Summarized? Articulate your expectations to the person you delegate to. Doing so will ensure professional, responsible, and orderly feedback. An added advantage: if written, the report can be easily shared with others.

9. Encourage questions. At the end of your explanation, encourage the person to ask any questions that may be still unvoiced. If none are forthcoming, do a comprehension check; have the person summarize the assignment as he or she understands it. You'll almost certainly need to clarify some details. You may even wish to "walk" the person through the task. This is a powerful, hands-on method for testing his or her comprehension of the job. Now is also the time to offer trade-offs if you get the it's-not-my-job reaction. Finally, summarize steps 4 through 9 in a brief, written memo to the person and, if appropriate, send a copy to your boss.

MISTAKE PROOFING

Providing Resources

When you delegate a task, you need to make sure the person has everything necessary to perform the task:

- *Sufficient authority to make necessary decisions.* If a certain amount of autonomy saves *you* time, a reasonable level of autonomy will save time for the person you're delegating to. Also, if the person needs to come to you for decisions, how much effort and time are you saving by delegating?
- *Access to all resources necessary for the task.* The person should not have to ask for access, one item at a time. That's a waste of time, for both of you, and not smart delegation.

Smart Managing

Meetings?

When delegating large projects, sometimes it's a good idea to have periodic meetings to assess progress. Be careful, however, not to micromanage via meetings or committees. Remember: the camel has been sardonically defined as "a horse built by committee." Any gathering should provide those to whom you've delegated a project with the opportunity to get a feeling for where in the process everyone is and to be certain that communication lines remain open. It should also provide you with a sense of how well the project is progressing and whether or not you should clarify any aspect.

It should not, however, be an excuse for you to reassert control over what you've already decided to delegate. Resist the impulse to take back more control over the project than you need.

10. Conduct unscheduled status checks. Relying solely on official status reviews can discourage flexibility as a project unfolds. Feel free to informally drop in on anyone to whom you've delegated. Be prepared to adjust procedures and goals as necessary. The worst-case scenario: you may even have to pull the project and find a new person to do it or do it yourself. No matter how well you plot things out, the unexpected is to be expected.

11. Evaluate results. Ask yourself the following questions:

- Did the person meet the deadline? If not, was it because it was unreasonable?
- Did the person achieve all goals?
- Did the person meet, exceed, or fall short of your expectations?
- Were there any surprises?
- Did the person realize the promised benefits?
- Was this the right person for this task? Would you delegate to this person again?
- Was the final report thorough?
- Was your emotional reluctance to delegate extinguished? If not, why not?

12. Praise/Suggest Improvements. Physically, it's not easy to pat yourself on the back. Emotionally, it's very easy. Delegating was an achievement for you.

If you succeeded, congratulate yourself. But also give credit where credit is due—to the people to whom you delegated. Their success doesn't diminish yours; it enhances it. If your own boss is wise, he or she will instantly recognize that.

What if things didn't turn out as well as you wanted? At least recognize the effort, suggest improvements for next time, and transform the whole process into a learning experience for you and for the person to whom you delegated.

Delegating is a subtle art. It requires careful thought and wisdom. Each solution to a delegating problem must match the needs of the people involved. Effective delegation is a key concept in time management. And it's an old lesson. (Consider this, for example: Santa Claus might have an easier job if he delegated some of those chimneys to elves whose small stature would be better suited to the task.)

But there's another important way to avoid unwanted or inappropriate work—learning to say "no." Is it really feasible? Yes—and Chapter 7 will show you how.

Manager's Checklist for Chapter 6

- ❑ You can delegate not only downward, but also laterally and upward.
- ❑ Delegate tasks you don't like but that others might like and tasks for which others are better qualified than you.
- ❑ To delegate effectively, get past the fear of losing control, of thinking you're the only person who can do it right, the belief that you'll look bad or that you don't have the authority to delegate, or the fear that you'll become dispensable.
- ❑ Follow all 12 steps to effective delegation and flowchart the tasks delegated to ensure that you and others understand them.

Learning to Say No

It's 7 p.m. You've settled down to a nice, quiet dinner at home. The phone rings.

"Hello, is this John Smith?"

"Yes," you answer.

"How are you this evening?"

"Fine," you respond, watching your food get cold and wondering who this is.

"As a fellow graduate of the East Overshoe University, I'm sure you've kept up on our recent successes. And you've certainly been supportive of our efforts to continue that tradition of quality. That's why we thought you'd like to know about our new fundraising drive ...."

Maybe you'd like to contribute to old EOU. Maybe not. It's hard to say no to this eager young voice. And you're even willing to forgive this interruption of your personal life and the manipulative way that caller has "reeled" you in.

TRICKS OF THE TRADE

Managing Mail

Here are a few tactics to help you say no to intrusions on your time through the mail:

- Throw away or shred any piece of mail that's clearly "junk." Don't even bother to open it. (Direct mail experts know this, of course, so they often put something that looks like a check behind the cellophane envelope window that makes you afraid *not* to open it.)
- Cancel subscriptions to publications you rarely get around to reading.
- Contact the Direct Marketing Association (1120 Avenue of the Americas, New York, NY 10036-6700 or www.the-dma.org) to obtain forms that can help you limit the flow of unwanted mail to your office or home.
- Skim all "wanted" magazines for relevant articles, highlighting or underlining key points. If you don't have time to read them, tear out important articles and file them for future reference.
- Discard any topical magazine that's more than a few months old. You'll never get to it anyway.

Telemarketers know that it's hard to say no. Indeed, they prey on our politeness—those dinner interruptions aren't just for the old alma mater but also for timeshares, opinion polls, investment schemes, and sales pitches for all types of products. Such calls have become so common that there are now companies that, for a fee, will work to take you off telemarketing lists. Now *that's* an investment idea.

It's not just telemarketers, either. Friends, fellow workers, and others often place subtle (and sometimes not so subtle) demands on our time and energy. If, out of politeness, we acquiesce to all these demands, we subject ourselves to draining levels of stress. The result: our performance in all areas suffers. Sometimes we just need to say no to those who make requests or demands of us.

Saying no is exceedingly difficult, though, isn't it? It takes willpower. Indeed, in an age when most people are already too burdened with obligations, to learn when and how to say no becomes one of the most crucial skills you can acquire.

What to Say No to

Robert Moskowitz, author of *How to Organize Your Work and Your Life* (New York: Doubleday, 1993, 2nd edition), identified two vital questions to ask yourself before saying yes to something you might feel reluctant about:

1. *What will this commitment mean?* Let's say you've been asked to serve on a committee. Before saying yes, you need answers to all the following questions:
   - When does it meet?
   - How often does it meet?
   - How long are the meetings?
   - What does it do?
   - What would my responsibilities be?
   - Are there any allied duties outside the meeting time?
   - How long would I be expected to serve on this committee?

   So, before you agree to do anything, try to anticipate any unvoiced or unexpected responsibilities that may emerge later on.
2. *If you had to take on this commitment tomorrow, would it—considering what you've planned—be a good use of your time?* Moskowitz considers this the litmus test of responsibility. When compared with your normal duties, does the project obligation seem worthy? If yes, then it merits your time. If not (and assuming tomorrow

Smart Managing

A Different Way

Of course, you don't have to do everything everyone wants you to do. But you also don't have to do everything the *way* everyone wants you to do it, either.

If you know there's a better, less time-consuming way to produce the same results, you should learn to say no to the approach others typically use. Be confident in the way you work best. After all, once you find a method of producing satisfactory results in your own way, you might be able to say yes to a request you might otherwise have turned down.

Saying *no* to the *how* may make it possible to say yes to the *what.*

is not the most critical day of the year), then maybe you should say no.

How to Say No

Psychologists have identified a four-step procedure that makes saying no safe, diplomatic, and effective:

- **Give a reason.** To simply decline to do something seems arbitrary, lazy, or irresponsible. If you give a good, solid reason for your decision, it will show that you're reasonable.
- **Be diplomatic.** Saying no can hurt, upset, or even anger the person to whom you're saying it. Tact is essential when turning down anything.

CAUTION!

Say No to Information Overload

We live in an age of information overload. But you can control how you receive and process information by focusing on what you need and rejecting what you don't. Here are a few tips:

- When reading a report, *read the executive summary first.* Skim what follows only to sift out necessary details. If you can influence the people creating reports, insist that they have executive summaries.
- *Subscribe to publications that summarize* facts, books, articles, etc. A few examples:

  Executive Book Summaries
  Wellness Letter (UC Berkeley)
  Kiplinger Washington Letter

- *Avoid real-time TV viewing.* Tape TV shows and fast-forward past commercials.
- *Use the bookmark feature* on your Internet browser to store information sites you use frequently.
- *Get a voice-mail system that limits messages* to one minute and doesn't record hang-ups. Whether or not you have a limiting feature on your equipment, warn callers in your outgoing message that they have 60 seconds to state their message. (Yes, they may call back and leave a continuation of their message, but the second attempt will be far more compact than the first.)

- **Suggest a trade-off.** If you explain that you're willing to find some other way to contribute, you'll underscore your goodwill. For example, if your boss suggests you do something and you're convinced that you're the wrong person to do it, explain your perceptions and suggest taking on another task that you know needs to be done.
- **Don't put off your decision.** "Let me think it over ..." is probably the most common way for people to postpone an inevitable "no." And it's utterly unfair. Be courageous. If you know that you cannot or will not do something, be decisive and *say* it, then and there. Delaying a decision is only justified in intricate situations.

An Exercise

Make a list of current responsibilities to which you probably should have said no. How might hindsight have made you do things differently? Does this suggest any resolutions for the future? One reminder: unfortunately, there are things you'd probably like to say no to that, for "political" reasons, require a yes.

> **How Not to Take No for an Answer**
>
> TRICKS OF THE TRADE
>
> Of course, the opposite problem of learning how to say no is getting others to say yes. The solution is persistence.
>
> In sales, the single most common reason for failure to close the deal is that the salesperson never asks for the business. The seller tiptoes around the question, never coming right out and asking the customer to say yes. And, when the first response is no, even those salespeople who bothered to ask tend to give up.
>
> You need to be able to say no and mean it, but you may have to be persistent enough to get others to say yes.

Dealing with Meetings and Committees

"A meeting," said one pundit, "is an event at which the minutes are kept and the hours are lost."

The average executive spends half of his or her week in meetings. Of this, about six hours' worth, according to several studies, is rated as totally unnecessary. Yet, in many businesses, meetings have become a ritual and committees are a duty, so that it's nearly impossible to say no to them.

Your job: to ensure that the meetings you attend result in a sleek, productive use of everyone's time. If you run the meeting, your task requires commitment to time management principles. If you're a participant, your challenge is more acute: to subtly guide the group to productive activity. Here are 12 guidelines that will help you increase a meeting's productivity.

1. *Create a written agenda for each meeting.* Make sure it's distributed to all participants at least 24 hours in advance. (Figure 7-1 shows a sample agenda form.) If you're asked to attend a meeting scheduled by someone else, request that he or she pro-

To ______	Meeting Date ______	
From ______	Start Time ______	
Mailing Date ______	End Time ______	
# Attached Pages ______	Location ______	
Topics to Be Covered (in order)	**Presented By**	**Time**
1. ______	______	______
2. ______	______	______
3. ______	______	______
4. ______	______	______
5. ______	______	______
6. ______	______	______
7. ______	______	______
8. ______	______	______
Key Meeting Objectives/Goals		
Premeeting Preparation		

Figure 7-1. Sample meeting agenda form

vide you with a written agenda in advance.

2. *Assign the meeting a clear start time.* Check for conference room availability. Equally important: the meeting shouldn't be delayed for late arrivals. Participants will soon learn that you expect them to be prompt. (Of course, leave room for exceptional circumstances or essential people.)

3. *Assign an official closing time to the meeting.* Open-ended meetings can drag on, with participants mired in trivial or ancillary concerns. A tight finish time disciplines participants to work more efficiently and with fewer tangents. Shorter meetings tend to concentrate discussions on the real goals of the meeting and keep it focused. If the meeting length must expand, it should be by the consensus of all the participants. And if the meeting was scheduled by someone else, ask that he or she set a finish time.

4. *Set at least one goal for your meeting.* A meeting without clear objectives is rudderless. A committee meeting should have a "para-goal." Concentrate on how the meeting should achieve the component objectives of that goal.

5. *Be reasonable about the number of topics to be covered.* Having established a start time, a finish time, and a set of goals, you should be able to designate a reasonable number of subjects for discussion. An agenda too tight with topics is doomed from the start. If you must cover a sizable number of themes, consider the following:

- Establish a later finish time.
- Postpone less important priorities to the next meeting.
- Divide your meeting into simultaneous or separate submeetings that deal with fewer topics.
- Create a separate meeting during which the whole group will tackle what cannot be covered in the time allotted.

6. *Invite only the necessary people.* People who plan meetings often feel they should invite everyone even remotely interested in what's going on. This is a serious mistake. The time it takes to get things done in a meeting expands geometrically with the

number of its participants. Be merciless when inviting people to attend. An observation: meetings and committees function best with six members at most. With more, the gathering becomes less productive and more of a forum for views. Generally, the true, often unstated purpose of such a large meeting is to protect democratic decision making (or, at least, its image).

7. *Never schedule a meeting because it's customary.* Many companies have the weekly "Monday morning conference." Many need it—but does yours? Or do most regularly scheduled meetings encourage people at your workplace to think up things to say? If so, it might be time to reconsider that tradition. In effect, you'll be saying no to an obligation that, ultimately, may have minimal value.

8. *Never require a group of people to work on something that one person could do just as easily.* Before you schedule any meeting, add up the hourly salaries of all participants and multiply that number by the projected meeting duration. That will sober you up. It will also open up alternatives, like canceling the meeting in favor of proposals that get circulated to all relevant personnel for comments.

9. *Create an environment for productivity.* Use the checklist of environmental factors (sidebar) prior to your next meeting.

TOOLS

Checklist of Environmental Factors for a Meeting

- ❑ Is lighting conducive to productivity and mood?
- ❑ Would a room with windows open up the space or lead to distractions?
- ❑ Does the configuration of the table encourage good work communication?
- ❑ Are the chairs comfortable?
- ❑ Is the temperature favorable for concentration?
- ❑ Are audiovisuals in place?
- ❑ Do drinks, snacks, and décor make the room user-friendly?
- ❑ Is the room free from all but essential interruptions?

10. *Establish an idea bin.* On a flipchart, transparency, or white-board, list all ideas that the meeting generates. Doing so can also guide the person who is taking the official notes.

An interesting variation: create a "tangent bin" flipchart sheet (tape it to the wall). All tangents should be listed on it and, time permitting, they can be taken up toward the meeting's end. This is a powerful way to diffuse digressions.

11. *At the meeting's close, orally summarize all agreements, assignments, and decisions.* Consensus is integral to a meeting's success. This is also the time for participants to pose clarifying questions, to fill out any details missing from the group's action plan, to reinforce accomplishments, and, if appropriate, to set the next meeting.

12. *Via a written meeting summary, list all steps to be taken to fulfill the meeting's consensus.* The Meeting Summary Form (Figure 7-2, page 90) provides you with a document to pin down agreed-upon efforts, assignments, and deadlines. In essence, it's a pared-down, action-oriented version of the venerable minutes. Figure 7-3 (page 91) summarizes the steps of an effective meeting.

If You're Not the Chairperson

All these guidelines for better meetings seem useful. But suppose you're just a participant? How can you get the person running things to do it more time-efficiently?

Perhaps you can volunteer to do certain things to facilitate efficiency. For example, you might offer to provide an agenda form or to take minutes and translate them into a meeting summary. Maybe you could suggest that the next meeting have an official finish time or that an "idea bin" would be useful. If you can't say no to a meeting, you can at least say yes to more efficient and vigorous meetings by using initiative and setting an example.

Meeting Title:	Attendees:	______________
Meeting Date:		______________
Chaired by:		______________
Recorded by:		______________
		______________
		______________
		______________

Actions Agreed Upon	Persons Responsible (Initials)	Deadline
1. ______________	______________	________
2. ______________	______________	________
3. ______________	______________	________
4. ______________	______________	________
5. ______________	______________	________
6. ______________	______________	________
7. ______________	______________	________
8. ______________	______________	________

Topic Postponed:	Next Meeting Date: ______________
	Start Time: ______________
	End Time: ______________
	❑ Last meeting's agenda attached
	❑ Next meeting's agenda attached

Figure 7-2. Meeting summary

Conclusion

To say no is difficult, but it's sometimes necessary. If you evaluate the ways you spend your time meeting and pursuing information, though, you can indeed learn to be discriminating and more productive. Another effective method of saying no involves learning to anticipate the unexpected. Forewarned is forearmed, after all. That indispensable art of anticipating is the subject of Chapter 8.

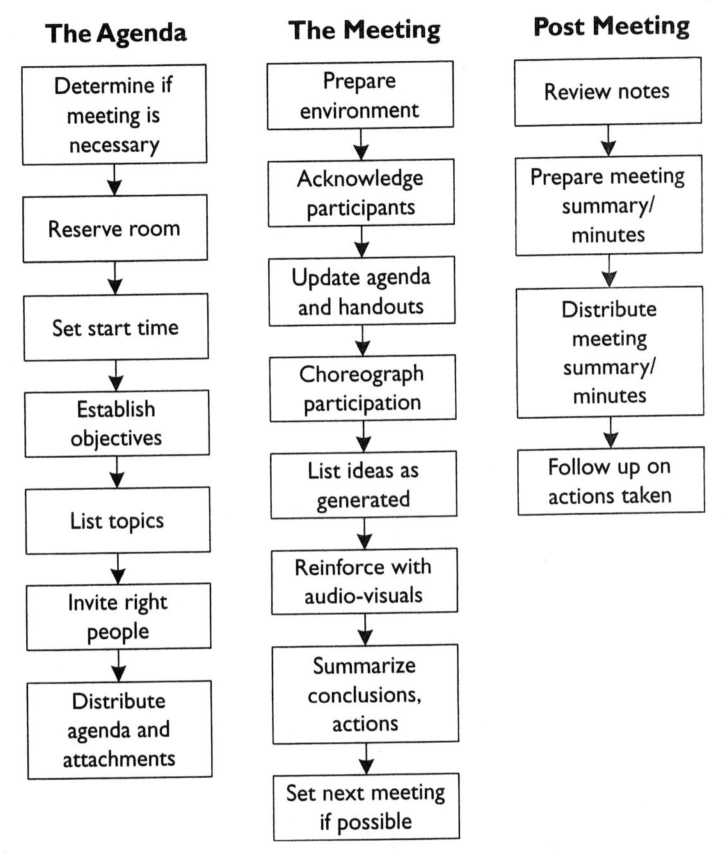

Figure 7-3. Flowchart for effective meetings

Manager's Checklist for Chapter 7

❏ Before saying yes, always weigh what your commitment will mean.

❏ When turning down something, give a diplomatic reason, suggest a trade-off, and don't put off your decision.

❏ To maximize productivity, meetings should have
- Agendas
- Clear start and end times

- Goals
- A reasonable number of topics
- The necessary number of participants
- Conducive physical environments
- Oral and written summaries

- ❑ Reconsider meetings or committees that are routine or "expected."
- ❑ If you're not the chairperson, use your initiative to help direct committee members toward greater efficiency.

The Art of Anticipating

In the 1950s America was flush with possibilities. The powerful manufacturing engines of World War II had finally been retooled to peacetime needs. Ranch houses, huge cars, jet airliners, freeways, rockets, and TV had redefined the face of America. Anything seemed feasible.

In the midst of all this gee-whiz optimism, a TRW engineer made a memorable and rather cynical presentation. The speaker recast a quote he had read in Aviation Mechanics Bulletin: *"If an aircraft part can be installed incorrectly, it will be." His new, generic version: "If anything can go wrong, it will." That engineer's last name was Murphy.*

Or so one of the stories goes. (There are at least five explanations of "Murphy's Law.") Not that the twentieth century was the first to note that "the best laid schemes of mice and men often go astray," as eighteenth-century poet Robert Burns put it. But as our lives have become increasingly complicated and reliant on technology, glitches appear to be far more prevalent

Smart Managing

Keeping Abreast of the Times

It may seem an obvious point, but the truth is that anticipating the future involves knowledge of both the past and the present.

You can dramatically improve your ability to predict upcoming events (and your chances of forestalling future problems) if you simply keep your eyes and ears open. The more you know about what's going on around you, the more likely you are to recognize when events are moving in a direction that might impact you.

For instance, gossip isn't always useless. If you've heard that your boss may be up for a promotion, you anticipate the possible changes. If she gets it, you may also be promoted. On the other hand, you may stay where you are and get a new boss. Either way, it's smart to make sure that you're ready and stay alert to signs of changes.

and pesky: cell phone calls disconnect, computers crash, people you need to talk to fail to return your calls. Confusion not only reigns, it pours. Murphy was probably an optimist.

But there's another, very old saying that embodies *the* tactic for defeating chaos: "A stitch in time saves nine." Foresight is indeed one of the most precious talents you can possess.

How Well Do You Anticipate?

Here are some examples of behaviors—some important, some trivial but telling—that characterize people with foresight. How many of them apply to you?

- They make a copy of every document they write or sign.
- They reconfirm appointments made some time ago.
- They keep a pad and pencil beside their phones.
- They keep maps in their cars.
- They keep service manuals for home appliances in a place where they can be quickly found.
- They have their cars serviced regularly.
- They're prepared, in case of sickness, to have someone at work cover their responsibilities with reasonable efficiency.

- They keep light bulbs in their homes to replace bulbs as soon as they burn out.
- They have emergency plans in place, should their homes be hit by a power outage or a disaster.
- They take reading material with them to the doctor's office. (That way, they don't waste time reading *Modern Podiatry*, *The Journal of Gastroenterology*, or whatever else lies about the waiting room.)

If you found that eight or more of these behaviors apply to you, you excel at intercepting problems before they occur. If you identified with four or fewer, however, you need to work at your ability to think ahead. You're currently at the mercy of the unexpected—and probably get quite stressed when things don't go as they should.

There are a number of areas where a solid ability to anticipate pays off. A more focused awareness of these categories can help you become more able to preempt setbacks.

The Parking Meter Syndrome

This must be your lucky day! You need to pick up that new laser printer you ordered at Eddie's Electronics Emporium. And there, right in front of Eddie's, is a parking space. You screech your car into the spot before someone else sees it. You pull out a handful of quarters and drop one into the meter. That gives you 15 minutes, which should be just about enough time to pick up the printer.

You go in, but there's only one salesperson working and two customers are already in line ahead of you. You browse—there are so many neat gadgets here. In no time, it seems, someone is ready to retrieve your order. But they can't find it. You wait. Your printer is finally discovered. You hand over your credit card. The approval takes a while to come through. Finally, the transaction completed, you head out to your car.

And there, on your windshield, is a $50 parking ticket. You check your watch and find out that the "quick in and out" has

MISTAKE PROOFING

Anticipating Airline Delays

Airline travel just isn't what it used to be. Flights are delayed more often, especially since the renewed focus on airport security. Not only does it take longer to check in for flights, but you never know when a real or perceived emergency 3,000 miles away will result in delays at your airport. It's no longer possible to assume that you'll make that meeting scheduled two hours after your flight arrives or that you'll make that return flight scheduled two hours after the meeting.

Since air travel so often takes longer now, many people are reconsidering the necessity of face-to-face contact. Technology provides opportunities to avoid air travel by offering teleconferencing possibilities that are almost as efficient as being there in person.

But if you do need to travel, you should anticipate delays. It's wise to have an extra change of clothing in your carry-on luggage, as well as work you could do to make any unscheduled stopovers or long waits in terminals productive.

taken 20 minutes. You resent the over-efficient parking enforcement officer—and you suppress that more honest, troubling thought: for an extra 25 cents, you could have saved $50.

The parking meter syndrome touches many aspects of time management. You know that you have a 10 a.m. appointment across town and that it takes 30 minutes to get there. You leave at 9:30—and a traffic jam makes you 20 minutes late. You estimate that a project will take nine days to complete, so you start on it nine days out from the deadline (or worse, six days out), then find yourself working late into the evenings. As the due date approaches, you rush the job or you ask for an extension.

The odd thing is that, in such situations and others, most people tend to blame everyone and everything else for the stress involved. It's the fault of the police officer, or the traffic jam, or those new, unexpected, and unreasonable demands that the client made that throw off the schedule.

There's only one way to defeat this self-deception: accept responsibility, assume things *always* take longer than expected, and act accordingly. You may even have to trick yourself into behavior change: set your watch a few minutes fast, for example, or write the deadline as a few days earlier on your calendar. Since reacting to time cues is often automatic, you'll act as if these false times are real. It's a weird phenomenon—worthy of a *Seinfeld* episode—but it's true.

How Long Will It Take?

This bears repeating: things usually take *longer* than anticipated.

It would be wonderful if you could foresee obstacles every time before they appear. But you can't. What you *can* foresee, however, is the probability that they *will* appear.

You should *always* attempt to leave "wiggle room" in scheduling each of your activities. If, by some stroke of good fortune, nothing arises in the course of an activity to delay you, you'll have a little extra time when approaching the next task.

Does this mean that you'll start showing up early to most appointments or finishing things prematurely? Possibly. But handing over a project to a client or to a boss early is an almost sure way to impress. And an early arrival will give you time to prepare, to relax, or to work on mini-tasks or readings. (Consider carrying a sheaf of such items with you at all times.)

The False Deadline Strategy

You now have allowed for potential problems in what *you* do. But how do you manage someone else's behavior? How can you boost the foresight ability of those you supervise, your colleagues, your friends, and family members?

Give false times and deadlines to people, but don't tell them what you're doing. If they end up needing more time, you can magnanimously award it to them. If they're on time, all the better.

One other hint: Saying, "I need this in an hour" or "in a few days" may prove to be too inexact. Strangely, "an hour" or "a few days" can be interpreted as "three hours" or "a week." Better to say, "I need this by 5:00 p.m." or "This must be completed by Friday, noon."

TOOLS

Inventory Your Life

It's annoying when the stapler runs out when you're assembling a series of reports needed immediately. It's even more annoying when you have to leave your office to fetch a new box of staples. And it's little things like running out of staples and paper clips that can, cumulatively, add up to unmanageable stress.

So create a list of the supplies you use regularly. Opposite each item, indicate how many you have *in your office*, immediately at hand. (If these supplies are provided by your company, indicate only the amount that are only a few footsteps away.) You should have, for example, a minimum of two boxes of paperclips, staples, Scotch® tape rolls, pens, pencils, etc. within easy reach.

Make it a point to keep your personal supply cabinet or drawer stocked and to keep a record of what you use. Then replenish stock to maintain an adequate supply. Stay ahead of the game and you'll always win.

The Pack-Rat Approach

Don't you hate it when you run out of stationery, can't find a bubble-mailer envelope when you need it, or have to use that last Post-it® that's all sticky with dust and who knows what else? So you set forth grudgingly for the local stationery store, the one you've visited three times already this week because you ran out of other things.

If people were a little more like pack rats, they could avoid plenty of frustration. You should have, at this moment, both at home and work, extras of almost everything you regularly use and need. An effective way of managing supplies is to keep a running inventory list. Buy at least two of anything you're replacing—three would be even better—and restock several items at a time, rather than waiting to run out of items before replacing them.

Gobbledygook

You call your travel agent. That trip you planned probably needs to be changed. Will that be feasible?

> *"Well," he responds, "according to my CRS, your PNR indicates that you have an outbound fare basis of KYE21NR but the return is a KWE21NR. So even though you have an NR, for $100 you can change 21 days prior with an MCO. But that will probably require you to change your whole FIT."*

Fortunately, travel agents are trained to avoid using their industry's gobbledygook when serving clients. But every now and then they lapse into jargon. Everyone does.

If you're speaking to outsiders, jargon will almost surely cloud communication and beget problems. (Remember: most people are too uncomfortable about revealing their ignorance to ask for an explanation.) Jargon can even trip up your fellow workers. Newcomers, especially, may not yet be privy to your industry's or company's specialized vocabulary.

Jargon interferes with accurate communication and creates problems that may take up valuable time later to correct. It's better to make sure from the outset that you're understood and that you understand the person you're communicating with.

To get a sense of how jargon may impact you, try making a list of 20 to 25 words, phrases, or acronyms that are particular to your business. Once you've done this, become fiercely vigilant in your use of these terms. They tend to confuse the uninitiated, muddy comprehension, and perhaps initiate serious consequences when misunderstood.

Gobbledygook can go well beyond jargon. Poor phrasing, foggy sentences, and snarled paragraphs can all short-circuit communication, leading to setbacks later on. Here are some guidelines for making your letters, memos, and e-mail flow more clearly.

1. Avoid the passive voice. When the objects come before the subjects, the mind trips over the intended meaning. The subject of the sentence becomes hard to identify. For example: "The procedures that were outlined by the advisory committee have been found to be acceptable to everyone."

MISTAKE PROOFING

Know Your Audience

One fundamental mistake many people make in writing is failing to take into account the reader. People respond differently to written communications and, these days, most people don't have the time or patience to read carefully.

People now want information in a quick and easy format. They want to learn right away how the communication may affect them. They want to be able to skim, looking for the details that are important to them, without having to read too carefully the information that they don't need.

Keeping your reader in mind as you write will help ensure that others get what you need them to know.

Recast into an active (and more intelligible) form, this sentence would read more easily as follows: "The advisory committee outlined procedures that everyone found acceptable."

Another problem with using passive constructions is that they allow you to omit the agent, whoever is doing the action. For example: "Any errors should be reported to the HR staff immediately."

So, who's responsible for reporting the errors? We all know the axiom—when everyone is responsible, no one is responsible.

2. Replace negatives with positives. *No*, *not*, *none*, and other words with negative connotations set off confused and counterproductive feelings in the reader. For example: "To not prioritize will not help us and will, unfortunately, lead to failure."

This would be better phrased: "To prioritize will help us succeed."

3. Edit long sentences into shorter units. As one expert puts it: "If you can't say it in one breath, it's too long." Consider this statement: "This personal organizer is not only compact, but it's also very complete and it has numerous features that will help you streamline your business-related activities, as well as your personal life, with the added advantage of being affordable."

This version would be more effective: "This compact and

complete personal organizer boasts numerous features to streamline your personal and business activities. An added benefit: it's affordable."

4. Be specific. Vagueness invariably spawns unsatisfactory or incomplete results. Consider this vague request: "Please see me soon about the project I assigned to you."

More precise so much better: "Please see me tomorrow at 9 a.m. to discuss the budget for the Forbin project."

5. Organize your writing via dashes, numbers, bullet points, bold print, underlines, italics, and punctuation. Too often, people have little time for patient, thorough reading of business communications. To "predigest" what you write for your reader achieves two results: it maximizes comprehension and it helps you organize your thoughts. Indeed, this book has deployed such organizational tactics throughout.

Here's an example: "We should for security establish a policy that no one can issue refunds in any situation unless the person is a vice president, manager, or supervisor."

This version would be far easier to absorb: "For security, we should establish the following policy: No one can issue refunds in any situation unless that person is a:

- Vice president
- Manager
- Supervisor"

The Wallenda Effect

As he was getting on in years, Karl Wallenda, the still-skilled patriarch of the famous "Flying Wallendas" family, opted to try one more stunt. He would walk a tightrope between two skyscrapers.

> **Keep It Casual**
>
> TRICKS OF THE TRADE
>
> A conversational style is usually best for modern communication. Everyone uses contractions ("he'll," "doesn't," "that's," etc.) in speech because they're easier (and quicker). The same tendency applies to writing. Unless your communication is intended to be formal, using contractions and casual language can transmit your ideas better. They help to "speed up" the reading process because of their familiarity, and they help make the act of reading complex material less intimidating.

Normally an easy feat for a professional tightrope walker, the challenge was made difficult by the breezes that were sweeping through the gap between the two buildings. Suddenly, a great gust blew Wallenda off balance. Observers reported that, as he stumbled, Wallenda could have easily reached out and grabbed the tightrope to stop his fall. Instead, he held tight to his balancing pole—all the way to his death.

Karl Wallenda was fatally dependent on the most important tool of his trade, the balancing pole. In many ways, people are equally subservient to their own tools. When the tools fail, helplessness and panic result. Yet often, backup procedures are well within reach.

Technological devices—unlike people—are dumb and unforgiving. They do not fix themselves. When they crash, that's it. So, it's vital that a backup system or procedure be in force to intervene. (The aerospace industry calls it "redundancy" and it's one reason aircraft are so reliable.)

For example, rather than get rid of that old IBM Selectric typewriter in your garage, keep it in storage in the event that your computer goes on the blink. How about that old, cheap, manual can opener? What happens if the power for the electric one goes out or the motor fails?

CAUTION!

Batteries

One of the most time-consuming and potentially devastating causes of electronic equipment failure is a dead battery. It can wipe out the memory of your personal data organizer or disable the camera you need to record those new label designs. An uncharged battery can make useless your cell phone or laptop computer or the radio you keep on hand for civil emergencies or natural disasters.

You should have a supply of batteries for all of your electronic devices wherever you use them—including your car and your suitcase. Sometimes, there simply isn't time to go shopping for a replacement. And if the battery is integrated into the device (as in a cell phone), carry the recharger with you.

The need for backup applies not only to hardware but to software, too. Spell-check systems, for example, promise error-free prose. People then fail two proof reed watt they right—and produce perfectly spelled, perfectly wrong sentences like the one you just read.

Create a "foresight action plan" for yourself, listing important items—from both work and home—for which you have no real backup. Identify the appropriate forms of protection in the event of failure and promise yourself to take action to implement these backup systems within the next month.

Remember, too, that the Wallenda Effect describes less tangible systems—and the people who run them. Are those you work with cross-trained? If someone is out sick, is there someone else who can handle what that person does? If *you* are out, does someone else have access to your calendar, phone numbers, and work in progress? Nothing sabotages a system more surely than knowledge isolation.

Bell's Blessing (or Curse)

Do you think Alexander Graham Bell could have possibly foreseen the implications of his grand invention, the telephone? Freed from its cord in the last decade, the phone permits us to communicate from anywhere: yards, cars, and in any city we find ourselves—from the same phone number. Bell would have been astonished. People even a generation ago would have been amazed. Remember the "communicators" on the original *Star Trek* series? Well, we now have them (and they look a lot less clunky, too).

The telephone may be the single most powerful and versatile time management tool. It saves time, travel, distance, and energy. It's an instant form of communication. It also permits technological cousins, like the fax machine and the modem, to ply their electronic paths. In a slightly different form, it allows interaction with all manner of computer knowledge and can access the Internet. Soon it will permit us to see the people we call, thereby overcoming its one great drawback: that it communicates aurally in what has become a visual world. Visual telephones will bring whole new dimensions to the conference call and to computer communications, using the greater speed and clarity of DSL lines—the high-speed "children" of the telephone line.

But used improperly—which is easy to do—the telephone can be a black hole of time. Here are six ways in which the telephone can drain valuable and often unanticipated moments from your life—and what to do about each of them.

Setback 1: Talking too long on each call. Two kinds of people inhabit this world: those who hate talking on the phone and those who relish it. In either case—and depending on who is controlling the conversation, which is often the person who made the call—more time is often spent on the phone (especially in work situations) than is necessary. A few tricks can help trim your calls:

- *Minimize the opening chitchat.* At least a little social talk at the onset of a call helps personalize what is to follow. But it can take time and divert you from your purpose. Be very aware of that initial socializing and keep it to a minimum.
- *Write out, in advance, a list of all the topics you intend to cover.* Such an inventory will help organize your conversation more efficiently. (This, of course, usually works only if *you* make the call.)
- *Take control of the conversation when someone else calls.* This is critical if the other person is poorly organized or gabby. If he or she seems stuck in the social opening, wait for a pause and say, "So what can I do for you?" If the business portion of the call moves aimlessly or runs too long, interject something like "Sorry, but I have to be at a meeting in five minutes. Let's try to wrap this up."
- *Keep a three-minute hourglass on your desk and turn it when you begin speaking.* This tactic, recommended by

time management writer Michael LeBoeuf, seems a little drastic. Yet it's probably a very effective way for some to discipline their conversations.

- *Buy a phone that tracks time spent on a conversation.* There's something persuasive about that LCD screen on phones that clicks off elapsed time. It's almost like a taxi meter. And like a meter, it reminds you that this call is costing you, both in time and money.

Setback 2: Forgetting what was said. Once spoken, words tend to evaporate. You think you'll remember what was covered, then later you realize that you have no reference to the points made or actions required. The solution is a telephone communications record, like Figure 8-1 on the next page.

The use of this form is rather self-explanatory. One clarification: in the "by" columns, put "me" or the initials of the other person.

Make copies of the document: keep them in a ring binder for future reference. They can serve to track a call's content, as well as map out a call in advance.

Setback 3: Misunderstanding the message. You've outlined your conversation, clarified each point, and even summarized to the other person what you agreed on. What are the odds that your message was fully and accurately comprehended? One study's conclusion: there's a 90% chance that your message will be understood incompletely.

You can do only so much to prevent misunderstandings. First, as discussed, outline the conversation, keep it brief, and make a record of it. But the best solution is to create a short follow-up note, letter, fax, or e-mail from your telephone communications record and send it to the other person. If there's any miscommunication (and if the person is responsible enough to read your follow-up), you're sure to get a call to straighten out the misunderstanding.

Setback 4: Being stuck on hold. The average person is kept on hold for 15 minutes a day and 60 hours a year. If you liberate

Date:	________	Person(s):	____________
Incoming Call?	________	With:	____________
Outgoing Call?	________	Address:	____________
Conference Call?	________		____________
Time Begun:	________	Phone No.:	____________
Time Ended:	________	Fax No.:	____________

Topic Discussed	By	Response	By
____________	____	____________	____
____________	____	____________	____
____________	____	____________	____
____________	____	____________	____
____________	____	____________	____
____________	____	____________	____
____________	____	____________	____
____________	____	____________	____

Follow-up actions required:

Action	To/With	Regarding
❑ Letter		
❑ Memo		
❑ Fax		
❑ Meeting		
❑ Additional Calls		
❑ ________		
❑ ________		
❑ ________		

Figure 8-1. Telephone communications record

yourself from the receiver, however, you'll be free to work on other things while you're waiting. A speakerphone or headset is useful here. Try to call during what you predict to be an off time. (Mondays, for example, are *not* the time to contact your insurance company or most other businesses.) This is also a way to avoid that related phenomenon, the busy signal. (An automatic redial feature can help you defeat this latter problem.)

Setback 5: Being stuck in an automatic answering loop. Remember the Minotaur of Greek legend and the maze in which he lived? It took Theseus to navigate it and destroy the monster. You shouldn't have to be Theseus to get through a maze of such convoluted directions as "For accounts receivable, press one; for sales, press two ...." But these days, you practically have to be.

Theoretically, automated answering systems provide efficient fulfillment of your needs. But too many of these "wonders" waste your time as you navigate their options, only to find, in the end, that no option meets your requirements and that no human being can be accessed to answer your specific questions. These phone loops create quite a problem.

If it's a number and a person you're calling for the first time, there's almost no way to get past this loop. Just work your way through the system. However, if it's a number you call frequently, do the following:

- Note the "press 1, press 2," etc., options on an index card, for example. The next time you get the answering system, you can press the button you want before the message states all the options. If the system is extensively branched, with each option leading to another set of options, this strategy will save you considerable time. One potential problem: a few especially stubborn systems will not let you hit a number until the recorded statement finishes.
- If you know a person's telephone extension, note it somewhere. (If your phone has an LCD and you have the person's phone number on auto-dial, you may want add the extension to the end of the main phone number, so you can see it on the display.) That way you won't have to keep going into the system's name directory.

Setback 6: Playing "phone tag." Phone tag is a fiendish problem. One study concluded that people spend two years of their lives returning calls. The average person succeeds in getting through to the person he or she wants only 17% of the time.

Here are a few tactics to consider:

- Make a precise time appointment to call the person.
- If someone reaches you via a second line or the call-waiting option, tell the person you'll get right back, specify when (e.g., "in 10 minutes" or "by 5:30")—and then hold yourself to it.
- Find out the person's schedule, write it down, and telephone accordingly. This works especially well for people you must contact often.
- Ask the person the best time to call—a time when he or she is free but least likely to be busy.
- If an assistant or receptionist says the person you want is on another call, ask if you can remain on hold. At least you know that the person is there.
- If the person is the type who deflects calls via an assistant, telephone at lunchtime or after 5 p.m. There's a good chance that the assistant won't be there and the person you seek will pick up the phone.
- Determine if the person has a direct, private line. Tell the person when you'll definitely be available.
- If you need to convey only a small bit of information, leave it with the assistant or on voice mail. Doing so will save you both plenty of time, since a live conversation will take much longer to convey the information than a bare-boned message.

Conversely, if *you* have an assistant, bring her or him up-to-date about what people may want to discuss with you. That way, the assistant may be able to conduct the communication for you.

The Ultimate Setbacks

These strategies will help you manage time, avert problems, and control damages. Such tactics take on more importance when dealing with vital documents.

The Telephone Log

TOOLS

Do you tend to use random scraps of paper to write notes on telephone conversations, reminders to call someone, or messages you receive? Do you tend to misplace these vital scraps and find yourself in a frantic search for them later?

A telephone log might just be the answer to your problem. Generic "While you were out" forms are available at stationery stores, but you might find it more practical to create one of your own—three-hole punched, perhaps, to be collected in a three-ring binder.

The information you record should include the date, time of call, the other person, who initiated the call, the purpose of the call, the person's number, and follow-up. You might also allow a little space for making notes of information exchanged. If you organize the log by date, you can also use it to jog your memory by filling in the preliminary information for follow-up calls under future dates.

When you lose your wallet, for example, you lose not only money but all the time it will take to replace your driver's license, credit cards, and other items. And if your home or office succumbs to some natural disaster, the consequences will be far, far worse.

Here are strategies that will limit the hassles you'll face if a catastrophe occurs:

- Photocopy critical documents, such as the following:
  - Driver's license
  - Credit cards (front and back)
  - Birth certificate
  - Passport
  - Bank cards and records
  - Checkbooks
  - Property deeds
  - All insurance policies
  - Wills
  - Powers of attorney
  - All other vital business and personal documents

  Put one set of these copies in a bank safety deposit box

CAUTION!

Insurance

Insurance is something that allows you to pay for peace of mind. It's a mechanism for minimizing the worst effects of unanticipated future disasters minimized by simply planning for them.

There are many kinds of insurance, though, and many ways to "pay" for them. One form of payment is by spending *time*, rather than money, to make sure that the worst disasters that could befall you won't be worse than necessary.

You purchase life and property insurance with money. But you can "purchase" the same kind of peace of mind with respect to other critical elements of your life that are vulnerable to loss or damage—through good planning. The "insurance" you purchase with your time can be as valuable as the kind you purchase with money. Backing up your computer files, changing the batteries in your home smoke detectors, or even having the oil changed regularly in your car may take moments you'd rather be spending elsewhere. But don't neglect these forms of self-protection simply because they require an investment of your precious time. They can, in the end, save far more time than they cost.

and leave a second set with a relative or friend in a different community.

- If these or any other important documents are on a computer disk, create a backup disk copy and a hard copy. Keep backup materials in another location, if possible.
- Photocopy every page of your personal and business phone books every year (or create a new one and keep the old one for reference). If you store this information electronically, transfer it periodically to a backup system.
- Photocopy your business card file every year. Again, if yours is electronic, create a backup copy from time to time.
- Consider keeping two organizers: the primary one should be detailed; a second (kept separately) would perhaps list only weekly or monthly activities. One might be electronic, the other paper-based.
- Develop two lists of equipment (see Figure 8-2) in case of burglary—one for home, one for business.

Property Record ❑ Home ❑ Business

Your Name ____________________

Items	**Make**	**Model**	**Serial No.**
Television	______	______	______
Computer 1	______	______	______
Computer 2	______	______	______
Computer Peripherals	______	______	______
Monitor	______	______	______
Networking Equipment	______	______	______
Camcorder	______	______	______
Digital Camera	______	______	______
Film Camera	______	______	______
VCR	______	______	______
Audiotape Recorder	______	______	______
Audio System	______	______	______
DVD Player	______	______	______
CD Player	______	______	______
Record Turntable	______	______	______
Receiver	______	______	______
Speakers	______	______	______
Laser Printer	______	______	______
Inkjet Printer	______	______	______
Answering Machine	______	______	______
Telephone	______	______	______
Fax Machine	______	______	______
Photocopier	______	______	______
Video Games	______	______	______
Other	______	______	______
______	______	______	______
______	______	______	______
______	______	______	______

Figure 8-2. Property record form

- Photograph or videotape all your equipment and keep this visual record in a safe place.
- Have personal equipment engraved with your driver's license number and business equipment engraved with your company's name and address.

Conclusion

Foresight is a valuable asset. It protects you from setbacks. It helps keep your organizational efforts on track. And it can enable you to plug "leaks" of time in your scheduling, preserving those moments for more important and interesting matters. That will be the subject of Chapter 9.

Manager's Checklist for Chapter 8

- ❑ Always give yourself more time for completion than you think you'll need.
- ❑ Set false completion dates for others to help them finish tasks on time.
- ❑ Stock or create backups for everything critical.
- ❑ Communicate clearly and you'll reduce the possibility for future errors.
- ❑ Don't become overly reliant on technology.
- ❑ Give special attention to your time management phone skills.

Plugging Time Leaks

This chapter will give you an opportunity to assess your instincts for where all that time goes.

Take the following quiz. Circle the answer you think is correct for the typical American. (Some of these statistics were mentioned earlier. See if you can remember them.) Then, in the blank provided, write an estimate of how much time you think *you* spend.

Where Does All the Time Go?

1. In the typical home, the TV set is on for how many hours per week?

10 hours	30 hours	50 hours
20 hours	40 hours	60 hours

Your home: ____________________

2. The average American spends how much time reading weekly?

1.2 hours	4.1 hours	8.2 hours
2.8 hours	5.7 hours	10.4 hours

Your weekly reading time: ____________________

3. Most men spend how many hours shaving during a lifetime?

500 hours	1,500 hours	3,000 hours
1,000 hours	2,500 hours	3,500 hours

Your estimate (if male): ____________________

4. In a poll, executives estimated how much time they wasted per week in totally unnecessary meetings. What was their estimate?

21 minutes	41 minutes	72 minutes
37 minutes	60 minutes	104 minutes

For you: ____________________

5. How much time will a person spend eating over his or her lifetime?

1 year	3 years	5 years
2 years	4 years	6 years

Your estimate: ____________________

6. How much time each day does the average American spend commuting to and from work?

6 minutes	26 minutes	41 minutes
17 minutes	33 minutes	58 minutes

Your daily commuting time: ____________________

7. Most people spend how much time per day writing and typing?

5 minutes	22 minutes	41 minutes
17 minutes	37 minutes	1 hour 15 minutes

You write per day for: ____________________

8. The typical person receives how many pieces of mail at home each year?

173	361	598
295	415	867

You receive: ____________________

9. Over a lifetime, how much time does a person fritter away waiting in lines?

7 months	2 years	4.1 years
11 months	3.2 years	5 years

Time you think you'll spend: ____________________

10. The typical American devotes how much time per week to religious/spiritual activity?

7 minutes	31 minutes	61 minutes
17 minutes	48 minutes	77 minutes

You spend: ____________________

11. Business travel has become a hallmark of many of today's jobs. How many hours does the average person spend on work-related travel per week? (Factor in that some people travel almost continuously in their work.)

1 hour	4 hours	8 hours
2 hours	6 hours	10 hours

Your weekly business travel: ______________________

12. Ordinarily, people throw away 15% of their mail unopened each year. It took how many trees to fabricate that wasted mail (for all U.S. mail recipients)?

100,000	2 million	100 million
750,000	5 million	2 billion

13. The average person sleeps how many hours per night?

5.8	7.7	8.4
6.9	8.1	9.1

You sleep: ______________________

14. About how many hours per week does the typical woman spend shopping?

2 hours	7 hours	11 hours
5 hours	9 hours	13 hours

You spend (if female): ______________________

15. How many minutes does the average person set aside each weekend for grocery shopping?

37 minutes	68 minutes	93 minutes
59 minutes	81 minutes	104 minutes

Your weekend shopping time: ______________________

16. Executives estimate that they average how much time weekly on unnecessary memos (both writing and reading them)?

17 minutes	48 minutes	1 hour 47 minutes
32 minutes	1 hour 5 minutes	2 hours 7 minutes

You spend: ______________________

17. Each week, how much time do most people devote to paying personal bills?

14 minutes	34 minutes	51 minutes
26 minutes	41 minutes	1 hour 10 minutes

You spend: ______________________

18. How many paid vacation days a year does the average American worker get?

5.1 days	7.4 days	9.7 days
6.8 days	8.7 days	10.1 days

You get: ____________________

19. How many paid vacation days a year does the typical German worker get?

6 days	10 days	15 days
8 days	12 days	18 days

20. The average person squanders how much of his or her life looking for misplaced things?

2 months	8 months	2 years
5 months	1 year	4 years

You waste: ____________________

Answers are shown on page 131

Any surprises? In some cases you probably guessed low, in others, high. You may have projected estimates from your own life onto those of the average American.

Any conclusions on why a gap exists between your experience and those of others? Has the data led you to make certain personal or philosophical observations?

Many of the answers to this quiz came from Michael and Robert Shook's fascinating book, *It's About Time!* (New York: Plume Books, 1992). It contains hundreds of other similarly intriguing facts. These surprising statistics should remind you of how easily time leaks from our daily existence. For example, who would think that we waste five years of our lives waiting in line?

In a survey a few years back, executives identified the six greatest time wasters in business. The following sections discuss these results and examine strategies that can help you meet each challenge.

Time Leak #1: Socializing

That the participants polled indicated "socializing" as the number-one time leak is quite telling. It suggests that:

- Many managers view socializing as a major drain on their employees' productivity.
- Socializing occurs more often than it should.
- Many workers probably feel guilty about their "goof-off" moments.

Yet an "all-work" day would be grim indeed. A study at the Xerox Corporation a number of years ago concluded, for example, that employees acquire more useful information during their coffee breaks than from the company's operations manuals. In many ways, socializing—in reasonable amounts—boosts job satisfaction, morale, and, consequently, productivity. It's not unlike exercise: where experts once believed that vigorous physical activity hastened the wearing down of the body, it's now known that, in moderation, physical activity does quite the opposite—it keeps our bodies healthier and our lives fresher, happier, and more productive. So, too, with socializing: in moderation it's a tonic that enhances the quality of work.

Of course, it's more complicated than that. Our need for daily playfulness is affected by:

CAUTION!

Monitoring Your Staff

Many companies have begun to monitor the phone calls and Internet activity of their employees. This is, of course, to discourage Internet "surfing" and personal telephone calls.

While it's reasonable to make sure that employees are spending their time well, sometimes such efforts, when taken to extremes, can have unpleasant side effects. Morale can be severely damaged if valued employees feel that their company doesn't trust them. Moreover, personal phone calls are sometimes necessary, given the long hours people are customarily putting in at the office these days. Even the occasional "surfing" break may serve a purpose—if it doesn't last too long. It may clear the mind between tasks or even result in an unexpected discovery of valuable information.

You should encourage your employees to use their time wisely and productively, but draconian efforts to ban all personal communications, socializing, and even 'Net surfing may actually backfire by eroding morale and, consequently, hurting productivity.

- The nature of the job
- The requirements of the tasks and other activities at the time
- A person's mood at the time
- What co-workers are like
- How much social interaction a person's psyche requires

How Gregarious Are You?

How outgoing you are affects the extent to which socializing is integral to your job satisfaction. You can assess your gregariousness by comparing your own preferences with the ones below. The most gregarious people would rather:

1. Attend a sporting event than watch it on TV.
2. Go to a party than read a good book.
3. Visit with friends than work on a hobby.
4. Watch a team sport like football than watch an individual sport like gymnastics.
5. Work with a committee of people than work on a project alone.
6. Go shopping with family or friends than shop on their own.
7. Take a cruise vacation than get away from it all on a near-deserted island.
8. Play cards with friends than work on a jigsaw puzzle.
9. Attend a networking business function than read a useful newsletter.
10. Give a great office party than master a new piece of office equipment.
11. Be a therapist than be an author.
12. Take aerobics classes than take long walks alone.
13. Play charades than play computer games.
14. Be a talk-show host than be a sculptor.
15. Talk on the phone than do some gardening.
16. Attend a convention than watch a series of motivational tapes.
17. Carpool than drive to work alone.

18. Take their lunch break with fellow workers than have lunch quietly alone.
19. Serve on a hiring committee than reorganize their files.
20. Attend a training workshop with numerous break-out activities than attend one that relies on audiovisuals and lecture.

If you preferred the first rather than the second option in more than 14 of the above, you're a *very* outgoing person. If you're in a task-oriented job, you need breaks for human contact; they make you happier and more productive. (But keep them brief.) You're more likely, though, to be in a people-oriented position. For that reason, you don't necessarily seek out human interaction during down times; a quiet moment may work just as well. Warning: the more outgoing you are, the more prone you are to counterproductive socializing. You welcome interruptions too readily and perhaps tend to drop in on others too often. You can still be gracious with people, but be ruthless with time.

If you preferred the first option over the second in seven to 14 of the above examples, your need to take social breaks is about average. Your willingness to let people distract you is typical. If you're in a task-oriented job, you should feel comfortable about brief socializing. It will enhance your day. If you're in a people-oriented position, you probably don't do a lot of socializing on breaks. Quiet time is what you seek and what will refresh you the most.

If you preferred the first option in six or fewer of the above cases, you're an introverted person. Excessive socializing is hardly a temptation for you. But you do need frequent short breaks to maintain your morale. You're probably in a task-oriented job. Occasional socializing is something that could benefit you, especially with people you know very well. A paradox: you could easily slide into too much socializing (e.g., on the phone) with close friends and loved ones.

If you're in a people-oriented job, you thirst for solitary goof-off moments, since frequent human interaction can weigh heavily on you. Your breaks gravitate not toward socializing but into daydreaming, secondary priorities, or introspection. Be wary of such behavior; it can subvert work just as fiercely as too much socializing.

Time Leak #2: Misplacing Things

Next to socializing, misplacing things—according to the poll—was the greatest drain on productive time. One estimate: about three hours per week are wasted trying to find "lost" things.

Of course, things don't really get lost: they get misplaced. There's a well-known prescription: "A place for everything, and everything in its place." Indeed, several industries have turned that dictum into profits, among them: office-, closet-, and garage-organizer companies, Pendaflex, and Rubbermaid.

Two work areas—when disorganized—seem especially prone to time leaks: your files and your desk. Filing is discussed more fully in Chapter 10. Here the discussion turns to that critical work region: the desk.

TRICKS OF THE TRADE

It Was in the Last Place I Looked!

Finding that missing file folder is no different from locating your misplaced keys. Where was the last place you remember having it?

Most people panic when faced with the prospect of finding a misplaced and urgently needed item. These three most likely scenarios should give you a clue where to look:

- You absent-mindedly set it down somewhere it doesn't ordinarily belong. In this case, it's most likely to be found *on top* of something else—unless, of course, you later set something down on top of it, which will make it most difficult to find.
- Someone else moved it, in which case you need to think who might have had access to it.
- You misfiled it or placed it near—rather than exactly—where it's supposed to be, in which case you need to search in the immediate vicinity of where it belongs.

Stackers, Stuffers, Spreaders, Slingers, and Sorters

Five "species" of desk users occupy the offices of America, according to Professor Emeritus Ross Van Ness of Ball State University. Which one are you?

1. **Stackers.** You create organized piles of everything. Each project or category occupies a discrete section of your work surface. Files probably also line your workspace walls. Hopefully, none of your stacks resembles a tower, an art object, or a piece of furniture.
2. **Stuffers.** You shove unsorted papers into drawers and file slots. Your middle top desk drawer—if you have one—is a repository of paperclips, teabags, business cards, pencils with broken tips, pens without ink, decomposing rubber bands, McDonald's napkins, your five-year-old expired ID card, and a 19-cent stamp.
3. **Spreaders.** Your desktop is coated with seemingly undifferentiated layers of documents. With time, the area may resemble an archaeological dig.
4. **Slingers.** You're contemptuous of desks and their limitations. You sling your stuff everywhere—onto chairs, countertops, and, when there's a lot going on, the floor. Your guiding question: "Where is there space where I can hurl something?"
5. **Sorters.** You carefully categorize and subcategorize items, then file them away where they belong. You may get so carried away with this process that your desktop is one great, empty rectangle.

Do you expect the sorters to be the heroes of this time management tale? Not necessarily. Sorters have a better chance of finding things quickly, but surprisingly, many spreaders can reach into their desktop heaps and pull out just the right document. Stackers, too, seem to know what's at each level of each of their piles. They often use color-coded folders to aid the process. Stuffers can reach right into the correct drawer and within seconds find the object they're looking for. Even slingers sometimes function efficiently: their keen motor skills enable them to remember where something was flung.

Conversely, in all five categories are people who misplace things all the time. No matter which type you are, to successfully navigate your desktops, you must follow a style that:

- Echoes your thought processes
- Aids the nature of your job
- Enables you to find something swiftly and without undue stress

If your style meets these three criteria, then keep your current approach. If not, it's time to consider a different way of organizing your space.

What Can You Do?

There are simpler and surprisingly obvious things that work for virtually every desk management style. Try some of these:

- Reserve the surface of your desk only for active projects and the supplies you use most.
- Small backup supplies (e.g., paperclips, correction fluid, etc.) belong in a top drawer. Only a few of each essential supply item go on the desk surface. For instance, you don't need a can full of pens on your desk: keep two or three there and put the rest into the drawer.
- Place your phone on the side opposite your writing hand. That way, you can take notes without the cord crossing in front of you (or get a cordless phone).
- Establish a tickler file in a bottom desk drawer. A tickler file is one in which a separate file folder represents each day of the next month. Behind that are 11 folders, for the months that follow. Just drop things in their approximate date/folders; each morning look in that day's slot, where you'll find items that need to "tickle" your memory.
- Make the bottom drawer a filing system for your most important documents.
- Verify that your desk is well lighted and that your chair is comfortable.

- No matter what your style, reserve a large open space toward the front middle of your desk and arrange other materials along the three remaining outside edges.
- Furnish your desk with an A, B, C in-tray and an out-tray (see Chapter 3, page 30-33).
- Behind the desk of Cathy, the protagonist of a popular comic strip, is something she calls the "doomed pile." It is, she states, composed of things that she's avoided, ignored, postponed, skirted, dodged, loathed, and procrastinated on. The only stacks on *your* desk should consist of sorted and essential things.
- Most secondary, reference, or non-active items should be moved away from your desk. A rule to guide you: "Out of sight, out of mind." If you want to remember that you have it or if you consult it regularly, keep it on a credenza, nearby bookshelf or counter, or in a wall-mounted "hot file." If you can afford to *ignore* it for a while, store it in a filing unit or cabinet.
- At day's end, clear your desk and prepare items for the next morning. This might be an impossible task if you're a spreader. For most people, though, a reorganized work surface brings a sense of control. It's a way to summarize the day's work and to preview what is to come the next morning.

One final caveat: although you may function just fine from what appears to be a jumbled mess, your boss, colleagues, and staff may not perceive it that way. If your work area appears disheveled, others may conclude that you're disorganized, overworked, or irresponsible. Is that the image you wish to project? So bring this book with you the next time you're at your desk and analyze your workspace based on the above criteria.

Time Leak #3: Forgetting Things

It's perhaps an apocryphal story, yet it speaks reams of wisdom:

A young physicist asked Albert Einstein for his phone number. Einstein picked up his university's phone directory, located his number, transferred it to a slip of paper, and then handed it to the scientist.

Bemused, the young man blurted out, "Mr. Einstein, you don't know your own phone number?"

To which the great thinker replied, "Why should I clutter my mind with something that I can so easily look up?"

Most people are constantly juggling all manner of mental odds and ends. You *know* you must buy three things at the store on the way home, but you get there and can recall only two. You have a nagging feeling that you're supposed to return a certain call, then you remember it, too late, the next day.

50% of all you hear or read you'll forget within one minute. If you can't easily re-access the information you need, *write it down*—in your organizer, on a full sheet of paper (to file later), on a checklist, or somewhere else you can access quickly. It takes much less time to make a written note than to search for a lost thought.

Time Leak #4: Commuting and Air Travel

If only your office were the only place you worked! But "office"

TRICKS OF THE TRADE

Maximize Your Memory

Some people remember numbers better than names, while for others names are easier than numbers. If you really need to recall something later and have no way to write it down—for example, the name of someone to whom you've just been introduced—it might work to use a mnemonic device to help trigger your memory later.

How do you remember, for example, that Frank James isn't James Frank? One way would be to remember that F comes before J in the alphabet. That's a mnemonic device. Another way would be to remember that Frank James is a forthright person. He's French (Frank). Or that he's not a hotdog named James—"James frank." Yes, it's silly—but if it works for you, that's what matters.

has become a portable concept. Increasingly, as part of an overlapping strategy, because of deadline pressures or out of sheer boredom, people work on planes, on commuter buses and trains, and while waiting in line. Indeed, one poll recently indicated that over half of all executives on vacation bring at least some work with them.

Is this good? Surprisingly, it can be. If you're doing some work you enjoy and not disturbing the people with you, then a holiday environment can, in fact, enhance rather than distract.

Air Travel

Air travel represents a major time leak for business travelers. To guard against time leaks in air travel:

- Select a nonstop flight over a direct one and a direct flight over connecting ones. Each stop represents a potential for additional delay and another opportunity for losing luggage. What's the difference between nonstop and direct? A nonstop flight doesn't make any stops between a passenger's departure and destination cities. A direct flight stops in at least one city along the way; there's just no change of planes.
- If you must connect, do so between flights on the *same airline* and in a city that usually has good weather at that time of year. For example, Chicago can have major snowstorms in the winter, but Dallas doesn't. On the other hand, in the summer, Dallas is more likely than Chicago to have thunderstorms.
- Use carry-on luggage to avoid wasting time at the luggage claim area.
- Consider buying travel insurance from your travel agent. If your flight gets cancelled, your luggage gets lost, or you have a medical emergency, such insurance can take on a value far greater than the cost. It also has a little-known benefit: most travel insurance carriers operate a 24/7 call center, accessed through a toll-free number. The multilingual staff can provide assistance and solutions that will

almost surely save you time and stress.

- Request a seat that has an empty one next to it. Ideally, your seat would be in a three-seat configuration, with the middle seat empty. Unless the plane is full, that seat has a good chance of staying unoccupied and can become a "desk" for your briefcase. Then at the airport, have the gate attendant check on that middle seat. If it's no longer empty, try to relocate to another seat that provides what you want.
- Think about seat advantages and disadvantages: an aisle seat (more legroom) versus a window seat (the view might serve as an occasional, welcomed distraction).
- Position your seat to maximize work. If you're handwriting things, get a seat that gives you elbow room on your writing side.
- Unless you're very tall and need the extra legroom, avoid bulkhead seats (the ones with no seats in front of them). They rarely provide any place accessible for your briefcase or bag.
- If the airline provides the option, use your frequent flyer miles to upgrade to business or first class, which will be far more conducive to work. Upgrading is especially beneficial on long flights. Upgrades are most available on wide-body jets, on Tuesdays, Wednesdays, Thursdays, and Saturdays, and at departure hours other than 8-10 a.m. and 5-7 p.m.

Commuting

Whether it's on a train into Manhattan or on freeways around Los Angeles, commuting has dramatically expanded the "dead time" required for work. Yet commuting offers many opportunities. The New Yorker reading the newspaper on the subway or the Californian with cell phone in hand—these images now come to mind when we think of commuting. Are these commuters killing time? Or are they enhancing it? Or even putting themselves in danger? (One study found that talking on a cell phone while driving was about as dangerous as driving drunk.)

The important thing: commuting shouldn't become an opportunity for workaholism. If you want to work on your laptop computer during a flight or on a train, do it. If you don't feel so inclined, there's no reason to feel guilty. (And if you try to do it while driving, you should definitely feel guilty!)

In a broader sense, the strategy for tackling potential time leaks, like commuting and air travel, is multitasking. Multitasking is carrying on two activities more or less simultaneously. One is inherently a "no-brainer," while the other is more lively, engaging, or productive. Examples:

- Eating while watching an instructional video.
- Bringing a magazine to read at the doctor's office. (Hint: make your appointment the first in the morning, when it's less likely that you'll have to wait.)
- Listening to a motivational tape while commuting to work.
- Filling out a form while waiting in line at the bank.
- Downloading a computer virus protection program update while talking on the phone.

One wonderful benefit to multitasking—it not only doubles your productivity, but also defuses boredom, anxiety, or frustration. The example of waiting in a doctor's office is a fine illustration. Normally, the wait seems endless. But it would certainly seem shorter when you're doing something else. In fact, you may be bothered that your reading is being interrupted.

A classic bit of useful multitasking: the portable to-do file. Many people create a folder of easy and brief tasks to complete: short readings, forms to fill out, and so on. They bring this file everywhere and work on it whenever they've got to wait.

Time Leak #5: Reading Time

It's sad when we think of reading as unproductive. Yet the executives in our poll rated it rather high among time wasters. Reading is an essential wellspring of useful information. And

CAUTION!

Dangers of Multitasking

Four warnings about multitasking:

1. Never allow multitasking to *distract you.* Sure, it might seem like a good idea to go through your mail while talking on the phone. Almost surely, though, you'll miss something—maybe important points the caller is making.
2. Never allow multitasking to *become dangerous.* Having rolls and coffee as you drive in traffic while talking on the cell phone is potentially disastrous.
3. Never allow multitasking to *become obsessive.* The feeling that you must always overlap several tasks simply fuels your compulsions. And many tasks will suffer without your full concentration.
4. Never allow multitasking to *intrude on others.* Be considerate when using those phones on aircraft seat backs or your cell phone in public places. They're a wonderful convenience, but the person sitting next to you probably doesn't want to hear your conversation.

until some other technology does it better, print media disseminate information like no other media.

Those polled in the study must at least, in part, have been grumbling about information overload, not the act of reading itself. Review the strategies given in Chapter 7, in the sidebars on pages 82 and 84. They'll remind you how skimming, highlighting, underlining, and the rip-and-read tactic can help you better manage your many reports, letters, articles, tasks, and other written materials.

Time Leak #6: Long-Winded People

This should possibly have been placed higher in our survey. (The number-one time waster—socializing— probably siphoned off some votes.) There are several procedures to use with "talkers" (a few of which we've already examined) that are both diplomatic and artful.

On the Phone

- Call long-winded people when you know they'll be in a hurry (e.g., before lunch).

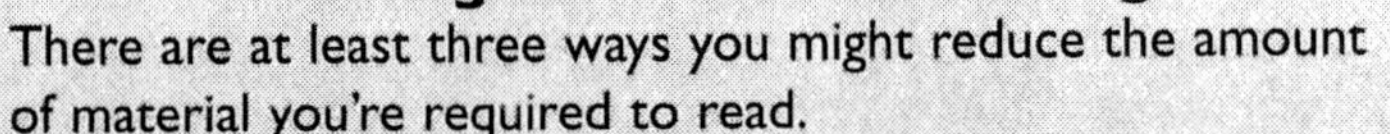

Strategies to Reduce Reading

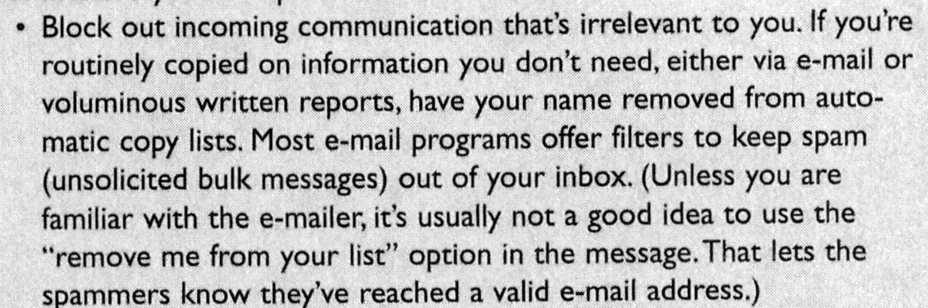

There are at least three ways you might reduce the amount of material you're required to read.

- Block out incoming communication that's irrelevant to you. If you're routinely copied on information you don't need, either via e-mail or voluminous written reports, have your name removed from automatic copy lists. Most e-mail programs offer filters to keep spam (unsolicited bulk messages) out of your inbox. (Unless you are familiar with the e-mailer, it's usually not a good idea to use the "remove me from your list" option in the message. That lets the spammers know they've reached a valid e-mail address.)
- Filter incoming material. Have staff or an assistant summarize or excerpt relevant information from lengthy communications.
- Delegate certain forms of information to staffers or assistants to read and handle at their own discretion.

- Outline your time limitations at the beginning of the call.
- Pretend to be interrupted by someone or something, then say, "Sorry, I have to go."
- Pretend you're calling from a phone booth.
- Screen your calls, then respond, if you can, via voice-mail, e-mail, or fax.

In Person

- Remain standing while you're at your workplace or in

Are You Guilty?

Are you one of those people whom others think of as long-winded? Sometimes you need to ask yourself some hard questions.

Many years ago, on *The Mary Tyler Moore Show*, one ever-excitable character had launched into one of her recognizably enthusiastic and long-winded stories. Another character listened patiently for a very long time and then, very gently but very meaningfully, intoned, "You know I love you, dear. But I must tell you. That was not an interesting story."

If you ever find yourself wondering whether or not you're going on too long about something, you probably are.

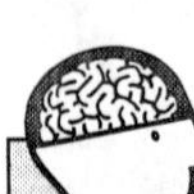

Drop-in Visitors

If you don't have an administrative assistant or secretary to intercept visitors who turn up unexpectedly, here are a few techniques you can try to minimize the time they can steal from your day:

- If you have a door, keep it closed whenever you need to avoid interruptions.
- If you work in a cubicle, post a sign asking not to be interrupted.
- Try taking your work elsewhere—an empty conference room, a nearby library, even a restaurant.
- Indicate that you have a minor emergency and ask for a time to meet that would be more convenient.
- If it's a colleague in your company who needs to see you, suggest you confer in his or her office. It's much easier to leave someone than to get that person to leave you.
- Say, "Can we wrap this up in just a few minutes?" This should provide a clue to your visitor that you're pressed for time.

your office; it will usually make someone else feel uncomfortable about staying too long.

- Outline your time limitations from the outset. (In essence, you're delivering a "time contract.")
- Stand up when you're ready to finish.
- Keep your body somewhat angled to the other person. This body language will convey your need to get back to something else.
- A surefire strategy: get up and ask the person to accompany you somewhere close by (e.g., the photocopier). Continue your discussion while doing your work there. When done, simply say you're glad you two talked, then leave the person there. For extremely persistent types, tell them you're going to the rest room ....

Conclusion

The phrase *time leak* certainly has a pejorative connotation. Each time waster, however, offers a corresponding opportunity. Those opportunities are accessible, though, only if you possess the right tools—and that's the subject of Chapter 10.

Manager's Checklist for Chapter 9

- ❑ Socializing, in moderation, can increase productivity. In excess, though, it can seriously drain your efforts.
- ❑ To be able to access things quickly is a powerful way to gain time.
- ❑ If it's important to remember, write it down.
- ❑ Overlapping tasks will help you offset time leaks.
- ❑ Don't allow long-winded individuals to hamper your effective use of time.

Answers to "Where Does All the Time Go?" Quiz

1. 40 hours weekly watching TV
2. 2.8 hours reading weekly
3. 3,500 lifetime hours shaving
4. 72 minutes weekly in wasted meetings
5. 6 years in lifetime eating (8 years if you eat a lot)
6. 26 minutes in daily commuting
7. 5 minutes per day waiting
8. 598 pieces of home mail yearly
9. 5 years waiting in lines
10. 48 minutes on religious/spiritual activity
11. 10 hours in weekly business travel
12. 5 million trees wasted
13. 7.7 hours in nightly sleep
14. 7 hours weekly. For men, it's about 4½ hours. Oddly, the more educated a woman is, the more she shops; the more educated a man is, the less he shops.
15. 59 minutes in weekend shopping
16. 32 minutes on unnecessary memos
17. 34 minutes a week for paying bills
18. 8.7 paid vacation days a year (U.S.)
19. 18 paid vacation days a year (Germany)
20. 1 year looking for misplaced things

Power Tools for Time Management

Imagine you're a secretary. (Yes, that term is becoming obsolete. But play along. You'll see why.)

Your first job today: to send out 10 identical letters to 10 clients. You insert two sheets of stationery into your typewriter, with carbon paper in between. You type the first letter, making sure you have the person's name, address, and salutation exactly right. Fortunately, you type about 80 words a minute, so you'll finish the first letter in about five minutes. Then again, you're not perfect; you'll probably make about five typos. But there's this wonderful new invention: a piece of chalky white paper that you can place over a mistake. Just type the same letters onto the paper, the mistake under it disappears, and then you type the correct spelling onto the stationery. So, realistically, it will take you about 10 minutes to do that letter and its envelope.

You follow the same procedure for the remaining nine letters, since each will be addressed differently. Total time for the project: about an hour and a half. These letters must get to their recipients soon, so you personally take them to the post office down the street to ensure promptness. Only a half hour for that. You're proud of yourself: it's only 11 a.m. and you've completed one of the most important tasks of the day.

Was that simple to imagine? Did something about it seem anachronistic? Oh, one thing we forgot to tell you—you were a secretary in 1950. If you'd done that task today, you would have typed the letter using a word processing program, corrected mistakes almost instantly, knocked off all 10 personalized copies in a few minutes, and then probably e-mailed or faxed the letter to ensure swift receipt. The whole process would have required a half hour or less, not two, and the results would look far more professional.

In recent decades, a broad spectrum of tools has arrived that enable us to manage our time better. Some—like handheld electronic organizers, cell phones, pagers, fax machines, voicemail systems, photocopiers, personal computers, and even VCRs and microwave ovens—are the offspring of advanced technology. Others are clever, non-tech artifacts: sticky notes, hanging files, correction fluid. But, like all tools, time management gadgets function well only if they're used properly.

Five Essential Questions

When choosing any time-saver, whether electronic or paper-based, ask yourself five questions:

1. Do I need it?
2. Do I need all its features?
3. Is it user-friendly?
4. How reliable is it?
5. Will it become outmoded too quickly?

By carefully considering your answers to these questions, you'll be able to assess how useful the device will be to your time management style.

TRICKS OF THE TRADE

Increase Telephone Efficiency

Here are some features you may want to consider for your telephone that can help maximize the usefulness of the tool:

- **LCD** allows you to view the status of various other features and functions.
- **Caller ID** identifies the name, company, and phone number of the caller, allowing you to screen calls and avoid untimely interruptions.
- **Memory dial** lets you store numbers you use frequently and dial them with a single button.
- **Conference calling** enables you to communicate with multiple parties simultaneously.
- **Redial** allows you to reach the last number called with a single button, so a repeated busy signal wastes less time. Some phones can automatically redial a busy number at set intervals.
- **Voice-mail service** is available through your local telephone carrier, eliminating the need to maintain an answering machine.
- **Call waiting service** permits a single phone on one line to receive two calls; alternate between the calls by pressing a key or the telephone switch-hook.

Other useful features or services are *voice-activated dialing, message-waiting indicator, call forwarding,* and *call transfer.*

When purchasing telephone equipment, ask about these and other features, and contact your local telephone carrier for details on the services it offers.

A Matter of Necessity

"Do I really need this?" It's the most basic, critical, and useful question a person can ask when considering a time management tool. Some people go out and buy every gadget imaginable, just because the devices are new or trendy. Then the item goes unused or (for a number of reasons that are examined later) drains time, rather than saving any.

In order to determine whether a time management tool is right for your home or business, you need to weigh its probable benefits against its potential drawbacks. For example, here are some benefits to fax technology, something that's been around long enough for almost everyone to be familiar with:

- Near-instant transmission of print.

- Reduces need to mail documents.
- Transmission can occur during phone conferences, permitting immediate feedback.
- Communicates to the recipient a sense of urgency or immediacy.
- Usually easy to use.
- Can serve as an adequate photocopier.
- Can be interfaced with other technologies (e.g., a personal computer).

Some drawbacks you may or may not have thought about:

- Requires a dedicated line, unless use is so limited it can share phone line.
- Glitches occur frequently.
- Loading documents can be slow without a self-feeder, which most machines have now.
- Controls in sophisticated units are complicated.
- Imposes expectations of rapid response.
- May be rendered obsolete by e-mail and scanning technologies.

Investing good money should yield good returns. If the drawbacks outweigh the benefits of a product, then the cost may not be justified. A low-tech or alternate-tech solution may be better.

One thought: technology benefits a business in a not-so-obvious way—they bestow an aura of professionalism. It's hard to take a company seriously if it doesn't use e-mail, fax machines, word processing, or photocopiers or if the output of the fax and photocopy machines is of inferior quality.

Redeeming Features

Manufacturers and sales reps generally sell their machines by promoting their features, generally in overwhelming abundance. But the features of any product should provide benefits to the user. In selecting any time management tool, ask yourself two questions: "Which make or model has all the features I need without too many features that I don't need?" and "Will I benefit in any way from these features?"

For example, let's go back to the venerable fax machine. You might seek the following features, since they would enormously benefit your efficiency, productivity, and time management:

- Automatically feeds multi-page documents from a loader.
- Prints on plain, bond, letter-size paper, rather than thermal fax paper.
- Sends documents automatically to multiple stations.
- Stores text in memory when paper or ink/toner runs out.
- Memorizes frequently used numbers for one-touch or speed dialing.
- Time-delay transmission allows sending documents when phone rates are lower.

To find a fax machine that has all of these features would be marvelous. The problem: the Pareto Principle. 80% of your usage will come from three or four features. But a model with all these capabilities may also possess dozens—even hundreds—of options that you may almost never use. The additional functions add to the cost, could complicate operations, and will multiply the chances of something going wrong. You may even forget about these extra features.

You should also read research reports or articles and talk with friends before making a decision about makes and models of time management tools to purchase (see Figures 10-1 and 10-2 on pages 137-138).

Is It User-Friendly?

> *A true story. A teacher asks her first-graders to define the word* genius. *One student's response: "Genius: When you turn on a machine and it works." That youngster already understands that devices aren't always user-friendly. It shouldn't take a genius to figure things out.*

Along with technological advances come technological complexities. The Pareto Principle, which maintains that we get 80%

Item: ____________________ First-time purchase? Yes____ No____ Current make/model(s) (If applicable) ____________________ ____________________			Makes/models under consideration #1 ____________ #2 ____________ #3 ____________ #4 ____________		
Features most desired	Current	#1	#2	#3	#4
1.					
2.					
3.					
4.					
5.					
6.					
7.					
8.					
9.					
10. *affordability (lowest price quoted)*					
Comments:					

Figure 10-1. "The features I will need" form

of the benefits from 20% of the features of any product, has never been as true as it is today. Word-processing programs can format text in dozens of fonts, font sizes, colors, and configurations. But a personal computer often requires maintenance procedures, such as updating Internet security software; deleting

Item: *Inkjet Printer*	Makes/models under consideration
First-time purchase?	#1 *ACME 3000*
Yes____ No ✔	#2 *BETA 4500*
Current make/model(s) (If applicable)	#3 *THETA K60*
	#4 *GAMMA 932C*

Features most desired	Current	#1	#2	#3	#4
1. *high ppm speed*		✔		✔	✔
2. *quality of color in photos*		✔	✔		✔
3. *graphics quality*	✔	✔	✔		✔
4. *separate envelope input*		✔			✔
5. *compact size*			✔		✔
6. *low noise level*					
7. *minimum one-year warranty*		✔	✔	✔	
8. *multifunction capabilities*	✔	✔	✔	✔	✔
9. *Supports Macs*	✔		✔	✔	
10. *affordability (lowest price quoted)*	$179	$287	$315	$299	$265
Comments: *Perhaps should also price laser printers.*					

Figure 10-2. "The features I will need" form filled in

unused and obsolete programs, files, or other data that takes up space; and searching (sometimes for hours) for the answers to questions that can no longer be found in the hard-copy documentation that used to accompany the sale of all computers.

The more complex the tool, the more you have to learn in

order to use it effectively. And learning new systems can drain away valuable time that might be better spent doing your job. So, as discussed earlier, start by identifying the *reasons* you have for needing the equipment and then find the make and model that will allow you to meet those needs in the easiest way possible.

If you use your printer largely for text documents and correspondence, you won't need a full-color laser printer. If you do need a full-color laser printer (e.g., for proposals), you'll want to find one that doesn't require resetting a vast number of your computer's internal configurations before each use.

Complexity of operation almost always requires a proportionate commitment of the time and effort you'll need to invest in learning how to use the product. And your own skills and talents should suggest the level of complexity you can manage effectively without taking a six-month training course on using the product.

Dependability

When buying any technological tool, dependability is a significant factor. Every malfunction or breakdown wastes time. The following tactics should reduce the possibility of downtime and minimize the effects:

TRICKS OF THE TRADE

Determining a Product's User-Friendliness

One way to find out just how user-friendly a product might be: ask the salesperson to demonstrate the product's features for you—or to allow you to try them out yourself, then and there.

When you begin to shop for a product, take a list of the activities you'll need to perform with it and review each of these with the salesperson. Have him or her show you the simplest way to do things on the unit you're contemplating purchasing, and then what additional features might be easily incorporated to improve results.

If you find yourself quickly getting lost with the salesperson's explanations, you may either need a better salesperson or a different product. If you shop around and still can't find someone who can explain the product's operations in terms you can understand, the problem is probably with the product itself.

- Consider buying a maintenance contract with every purchase. Be sure that it offers a temporary replacement unit if yours must go in for repairs.
- Ask friends to share with you their experiences with similar devices.
- Consult publications and Web sites that assess product reliability.
- Try to have a backup unit or system in stock or in place in case of a breakdown.

Planned—or Unplanned—Obsolescence

Not too many years ago, consumers suspected that manufacturers deliberately planned for their products to become obsolete. The auto industry was a prime example. Models would capriciously change each year and automobiles would appear old within a short time.

Planned obsolescence is no longer necessary. Because of the speed of technological change, things become obsolete *without* planning. Such quick change is most obvious in the electronics industry, where things become noticeably smaller, swifter, and more powerful within months.

When you commit yourself to a new tool, do plenty of research and then ask yourself, "Will this still serve my needs and make me competitive in five years?"

It will be a hard question to answer because it's impossible to know everything that's on the technological horizon. But the question will force you to project your needs and research the product. And articles appear constantly that attempt to predict the near and not-so-near future, so you won't be entirely without guidance in answering the question.

The Basic Hardware

There are certain technological tools that almost no business can do without in today's environment: the telephone, of course (and voice mail), the personal computer (together with software, modems, scanners, and printers), fax machines, pagers, and personal organizers.

We've already discussed telephones, voice mail, and fax machines. Let's examine some of the features of two other basic devices that offer significant timesaving advantages but may also consume valuable time: the personal computer and personal organizers.

Personal Computers

Personal computers are essential for business. The big question is what kinds of programs you need and how you can use the computer to manage your time better.

Here are some important tips for making your computer work for you:

- **Use a data compression program.** Software programmers keep upping the memory requirements with

Internet Research

The Internet is an astonishing research resource, but most people require some practice before being able to find what they're looking for.

In addition to ubiquitous news resources—including cable and network sources, newspapers, etc.—you can find Web sites for most major corporations and many smaller businesses. Most vendors provide product information and other useful data and take orders online. There are also university sites, profit and non-profit organizations, and countless other sources of information.

Your Internet service provider has a home page with standard information and a search function. Simply enter a word or combination of words and the browser will display page after page of sites that contain these words. An "Advanced Search" option available on most browsers makes searching more efficient, because you can identify specific phrases or word combinations to use or to ignore.

With a little practice, you can become an expert at Internet research. Two things to remember, however:

- **The Internet is seductive.** It can save you time—or it can gobble up time, since you can easily get drawn into site after site. Be disciplined: save your "surfing" for leisure time.
- **Not everything on the Internet is true.** Consider the source—and rely on information only from sources that you can trust.

each product update. If your hard drive is small, data compression programs can come to your rescue. They *shrink* the size of your files, essentially doubling the capacity of your hard drive.

- **Upgrade your software.** But do this only with the software you use frequently. You probably don't need all of the new tricks for every program you use. But you should absolutely take advantage of improvements in those programs you can't live without.
- **Buy the best printer you can afford.** But don't select one with features you don't need. If you don't require a color printer, a black-and-white laser printer will create the most professional-looking documents much more quickly than any inkjet printer—and probably at a lower cost per page. If you need color, inkjet printers—for now—are slower, but far more affordable and less complicated than color laser printers.
- **Buy the best-quality and largest monitor you can afford.** Computer monitors can be hard on the eyes, but the best ones—and the largest ones—make viewing a screen for hours at a time much less taxing. Flat-screen monitors may give you more desk space for other things and they consume less power, but they cost a lot more.
- **High-speed Internet connections can be very valuable.** Even if you use the Internet only for e-mail, a high-speed connection can be important. Those extra 10 seconds or so you might have to wait for your large e-mail messages to go out or come in on a dial-up line can really add up.
- **Increase memory and hard drive space.** It's surprising how much faster your computer operates when it has lots of available memory and plenty of space on the hard drive.

Having the right equipment is important, but knowing how to use it is equally critical to making the most of its timesaving features. Here are some tips for using your computer and its accessories to maximize your productivity:

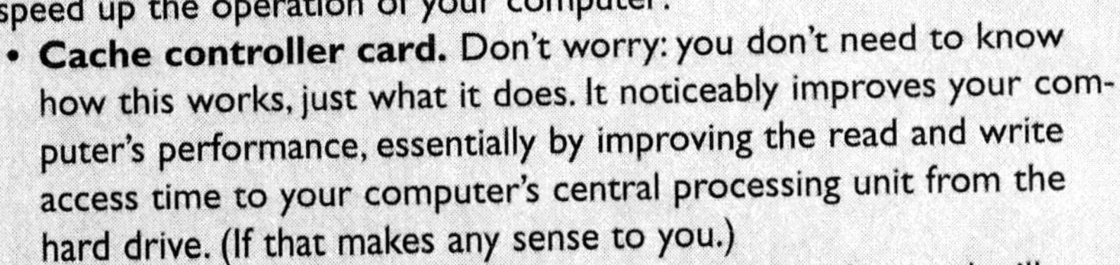

Some Useful Computer Accessories

Here are a few optional items that can do wonders to speed up the operation of your computer:

- **Cache controller card.** Don't worry: you don't need to know how this works, just what it does. It noticeably improves your computer's performance, essentially by improving the read and write access time to your computer's central processing unit from the hard drive. (If that makes any sense to you.)
- **Upgrade your video card.** The best available video card will provide amazing speed—particularly with graphics programs.
- **Cable, DSL, or T1 data line.** These are Internet connections that provide far faster transmission speeds than traditional modems operating over telephone lines. They've become more cost-competitive in recent years and may save you huge amounts of time if you use the Internet frequently.

- **Delete unused files and folders.** If you know that you'll never have to refer to a document or collection of documents again, eliminate it. Not only will this free up space on your hard drive, but it will lessen the number of files and folders you have to search through for what you need. There will also be fewer files for your virus protection program to scan, resulting in shorter scan times.
- **Back up your data.** Saying this once isn't enough. So, here goes, again: **back up your data.** You could, for various reasons, lose everything on your hard drive in a moment. Also, make it a habit to use the *save* function regularly while working on a document. Should a computer failure occur, all changes since the last save will almost certainly be lost. This applies not only to your desktop computer, but to your laptop and electronic organizer, as well.

  Several methods are available for backup: zip disks, CDs, and external hard drives. Your company should have a policy regarding which type to use. But it's up to you to take advantage of the protection offered by backup systems.

- **Install only the software you need.** Every program installed takes up valuable space and slows the performance of your computer. Most computers now come with an assortment of programs already installed—many of which you'll never use. Remove programs you know you'll never use; if you can't do this yourself, find someone who can. (This will leave room for a time-wasting game or two, which you'll have to resist at a later date.)
- **Learn the basics of the programs you use frequently, but don't get caught up with features you don't need.** Program designers are sometimes tempted to include features in new products just because they can. Many of these features are realistically useful only to a relative handful of people, but the rest of us get to pay for them anyway. They also exercise a kind of irresistible fascination for some people, who then spend hours exploring the possibilities of a new program—or even an old one that they suddenly discover can do things previously unrecognized. Resist the temptation to become too expert in the use of any program. There's often a seductive self-deception involved in learning how to invent 600 new page borders that will do nothing to make you more productive or save time.

Electronic Mail

Usually known as *e-mail,* this enormously convenient technological development has become both a blessing and a curse. Anyone who's ever taken a two-week vacation and returned to find over 1,000 e-mails in the inbox understands the curse. The blessing, of course, is near-instant communication.

In order to at least maintain a time-managing balance between the advantages and the disadvantages of e-mail, here are some ideas:

- **Don't use e-mail for situations that require a "loop" of gives and takes.** For example, trying to set up an appoint-

Smart Managing

Your E-mail Address and Spam

You're going to get spam—unsolicited bulk e-mail messages. You'll have to delete quantities of sales pitches, one message at a time—unless you want to delete the important messages along with them.

Remember: it isn't necessary to provide your e-mail address to everyone you know. Be selective. When you purchase anything or fill out a registration form on-line, check to see if you'll be added to the company's e-mail list. Make sure to read the Web site's privacy policy on sharing lists with other companies. And when you receive unwanted e-mail from a company you know, be certain to get your address removed from the mailing list.

Many states have laws requiring that anyone who sends unsolicited messages *must* respond to requests to remove your address from their lists. If a sender refuses, call your state's attorney general's office and file a complaint. Then send a copy of the complaint to the sender. That may be enough to get action (assuming that your state is aggressive about fighting spam). A federal law may also soon be enacted to curb excess unwanted e-mail.

ment with a colleague might take a series of messages: you suggest a date, your colleague counters with a different date, and so on. Use the telephone for such situations.

- **Be brief.** One e-mail per topic is usually best. Concise—even incomplete—sentences are most effective. Because many people receive a flood of e-mail messages, lengthy communications won't get the attention they may deserve.
- **Your subject line should be clear and command attention.** Again, unless the recipient is interested in the message immediately, which generally depends on the subject line, he or she may delete your e-mail without reading it. Don't make the subject heading too cute, though. That's sometimes the mark of a virus-carrying e-mail.
- **If it's urgent, pick up the phone first.** Most people don't respond to e-mail the moment they get it. If you don't reach them by phone, send that e-mail and back it up with a fax.

- **Don't "shout."** An Internet etiquette has evolved that customarily interprets words typed in all capital letters as shouting. (Not only that, but messages in all caps are harder to read for most people.) Italics and bolds, used sparingly, are better for emphasis. Unnecessary "urgent" message icons are extremely annoying, too.
- **Copy only those who need to know.** It takes so little time and effort to copy a message—but if the added recipients don't need the message, you're just cluttering their inboxes.
- **Send long messages as file attachments,** rather than putting the bulk of the information in the body of the message. Use the e-mail as a cover letter, to summarize the content of the file and indicate any action needed.
- **Check your e-mail regularly, but not constantly.** Depending on the quantity and urgency of e-mail you receive, once an hour to twice a day might be sufficient for you. Above all, don't become obsessive about reading each e-mail as soon as it arrives. That may interrupt the flow of your work and thoughts.
- **Protect your in-box.** Use software to filter out unsolicited messages (spam) and redirect them to a "junk" folder.
- **Print out critical information only.** If, for example, a colleague e-mails you her flight arrival time, make a note of it in your calendar; don't print out the e-mail. It wastes paper and it may later waste your time, as you try to find it. However, if you must compare multiple e-mail documents, printing them out may be easier and faster than working from multiple windows.
- **Become friends with the delete key/icon.** Most electronic messages deserve to be *trashed.* Otherwise, *forward* it, *act* on it, or *file* it.
- **Answer questions by inserting responses into the body of the message.** This spares the recipient the inconvenience of visually jumping up and down in the message. But tell him or her at the beginning of your reply that you're doing this.

- **In certain situations, phone calls or letters are preferable to e-mail.** Among these are very important messages, confidential or controversial information, communications that might be misunderstood, and important thank-you notes.
- **Check the spelling and grammar of all outgoing e-mail.** Use the program's spell-checker (and grammar-checker, if any), then reread the message to see if the checker(s) missed anything. Misspellings and grammatical errors make any communication seem less professional.
- **Use e-mail with people who tend to be long-winded on the phone.** You may have to wade through a ton of words for the substance, but at least you can do it at your own speed and convenience—and you won't have to waste time doing any polite small talk yourself.
- **Use auto-response to notify e-mailers when you're on the road or on vacation.** Check your messages only occasionally (if at all) in either situation, unless major negative consequences would result.
- **Declare a weekly e-mail-free day.** Weekends seem best for this. Hold back from checking your e-mail, say, on Sundays.

Personal Digital Assistants

Unlike the telephone, the fax machine, and the computer, the personal organizer is a matter of personal choice. Many people prefer a paper-based organizer; others may favor an electronic one, with communication access—sometimes with wireless Internet connection—through cell phone and laptop computer. The best known of these devices is the Palm Pilot brand, but there are others on the market, each with similar but slightly different features, advantages, and disadvantages. A generic term for these tools is the *PDA—personal digital assistant.*

For many people, electronic personal organizers are indispensable tools. Here are the most common reasons cited for using one:

- **Compact size.** You can carry your organizer everywhere and use it with a minimum of effort in almost any situa-

CAUTION!

Five Common E-Mail Mistakes

We know how rushed you are. But simple mistakes can result in more time lost than it would have taken to do the job correctly. Here are five common, time-wasting mistakes people make when sending out e-mail:

1. **Incorrect addresses.** This is the greatest cause of missed e-mails and the easiest to correct. Use the address book in your e-mail program. Simply add names and addresses the first time you send someone an e-mail and, after that, you'll only need to type the first few letters of the name and let the program fill in the correct address.
2. **Misleading subject lines.** To get noticed among the dozens of spam messages that clutter most inboxes, your subject line should make it clear that your message is *not spam.* If your message is deleted, you waste the time you put into writing it—and you lose time waiting for a reply that never comes.
3. **Inappropriate content.** Never use e-mail to break bad news ("We regret to inform you ...") or as a substitute for genuine human contact, when thoughtfulness is what's called for. Phone calls are always more appropriate than e-mail for thank-you notes, birthday wishes, and personal invitations.
4. **Emotionally charged and hasty responses.** It's so easy, in a flash of anger, to send someone a nasty e-mail—and then instantly regret it. Hasty, emotional replies have damaged business deals and relationships, requiring time and effort to restore.
5. **Inappropriate copying.** It's a bad idea to send information to people who don't need it. It's *really* bad to send information accidentally to someone who shouldn't see it. It can take a lot of time and an effort to patch the damage—if it's possible to do so.

tion. Expect organizers to get even thinner, too.

- **Scheduling capability.** For sure, this is the real power of the device, allowing for scheduling events and appointments, with adequate storage for related information and with flexibility in recording rescheduling that can only be duplicated in paper-based systems by means of a pencil and eraser.
- **Database and address book capability.** Most of these organizers have multiple fields and all allow editing with

ease and efficiency. Single search capability makes it easy to locate an address or a phone number. And some models even allow you to enter data via a business card scan.

- **Cut, copy, and paste functions.** These can make Post-it® notes to yourself obsolete. You can move any information from one section of your organizer to another with a click or two.
- **Search capability.** You can search all segments of the device's memory for information when you can't remember exactly where you stored it.
- **Expense records section.** In many models, this is extremely flexible, allowing you to set up various kinds of systems for keeping track of your business and personal expenses.

The most commonly cited disadvantages of electronic personal organizers are:

- **Insufficiently bright display.** This makes reading the display difficult for some. Newer models seem to be much improved in this respect.
- **Insufficient battery power.** The greatest danger with these devices is a battery failure. Many are powered by AAA batteries. Newer models have recharging capability.
- **Different backup systems.** There exist a variety of means for backing up data on PDAs—and not all of them are convenient or easy. Most require hookup to your computer via a serial port. The more sophisticated—and expensive—varieties allow transfer of data between computer programs and the PDA directly. You need to research this function carefully before buying, because if it's not easy or convenient to back up your data, you're unlikely to do it as often as you should.
- **Sometimes more time-consuming than paper-based organizers.** First, you have to turn the PDA on. Then, you need to key in the file you're looking for. Entering data can be slow and awkward, as most organizers have very

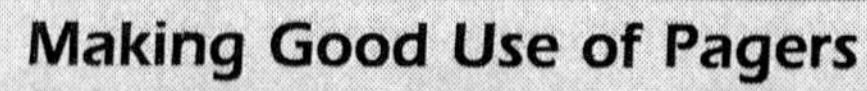

Making Good Use of Pagers

Most people know how these work, but here's a good review.

In order to page you, the caller keys in a special telephone number and then either a numeric callback phone number or an alphabetic message. The message is immediately forwarded to your pager, usually alerting you to the new message by a vibration or sound.

Many of these devices also access Internet news, e-mail, and stock quotes.

What's the point of a pager if you have a cell phone? The most important reason has to do with battery usage. When a cell phone is on but not in use, the battery can run down very quickly. A pager's battery lasts much longer, so you can let your pager alert you to the need to call someone and use your cell phone's battery only when making the call. Pagers also tend to get better reception in buildings than cell phones, so you're much less likely to miss a call when you rely on your pager.

tiny keyboards. This can be simply a matter of taste: some people prefer the tiny keyboard to writing. Others find PDAs difficult to learn to use, unnecessarily complex, and awkward to work with.

The electronic assistant—in one form or another—is here to stay. As with most time-management tools, a PDA should fit snuggly into your personal organizing style. If you've tried PDAs and, after enough practice, still feel more comfortable with a paper-based system, then go for it.

Remember: this information is current as this book goes to print. Within less than a year, changes may occur that will render obsolete some of these facts. Before buying any technological time management device, it's always best to research thoroughly, weigh advantages and disadvantages, and assess how user-friendly it's likely to be.

Soft Tools

Up to this point, this chapter has largely examined the time management potential of technological tools. But much of what we use to shape time is decidedly low-tech. A stunning yet modest example: the 3 x 5 index card. Cards can be used to ask questions, underscore problems, and pass along information.

In planning large troop movements, the U.S. Armed Forces—as high-tech as they have become—still often use index cards rather than e-mail. Why?

- Their size encourages concision.
- They're supremely portable.
- They're more emphatic and action-provoking than a screen full of letters and numbers.
- Since they're handwritten, they underscore open communication and commitment.

Paper-based communication, of course, can too easily encourage excess. Indeed, electronic communication is often lauded as *the* way to eliminate paper and all its inherent drawbacks. Still, "hard copy" will always be around. Here are a few ways to save "paper time" and curb the proliferation of paper:

- Rely on paperless management computer programs and be frugal in generating hard copy.
- Write your reply to a memo directly on the memo.
- Photocopy only essential items, but do photocopy and file elsewhere any item that would cause you problems if it were lost. This applies to e-mail printouts, too.
- Use Post-it® notes instead of full-page notes.
- Create labels preprinted with common addresses to save typing time.
- Imprint your most-used forms (such as invoices) with all the standard rules and regulations. Why type "Due and payable within 30 days" each time you send a bill, when this could be printed on the standard billing form?
- Use carbonless forms to save photocopy or printout time.
- Recycle paper whenever possible.

Paper-Based Personal Organizers

Nowhere is user-friendliness more critical—and more often

ignored by purchasers—than in personal organizers. Personal organizers are supposed to be just that: personal. They must serve the person, rather than obliging the person to contort his or her time management to fit the layout of an organizer bought casually.

If you like paper-based organizers, spend plenty of time comparing various models. Try to sense which one fits your style. Think about whether you need one that:

- Shows a single day per page, a week across two pages, a month across two pages, or some combination.
- Lists hour (or even quarter-hour) increments down the daily page.
- Is laid out in a book-size configuration (e.g., 8 inches by 10 inches), a narrow, "slim" format (e.g., 3 inches by 7 inches), or a mini-size (e.g., 2 inches by 3 inches).
- Is formatted as a ring binder, permitting supplementary inserts.

If you prefer electronic organizers, make sure that they're at least as handy as the paper-based kind.

Filing for Your Job

Filing—it's one of the great arts of time management. A well-conceived filing system will permit you to store documents efficiently and retrieve them straight away. There are several systems, each best suited to a particular purpose:

- **Desk files** are for the most important items.
- **Rolling cart files** are for important, self-contained projects.
- **Hot files**, possibly mounted on the wall, are for current items you consult frequently.
- **Cabinet files** should be reserved for items of secondary importance.
- **Storage files**, including box files, are for documents that you don't expect to refer back to except in an emergency.
- **Self-contained accordion files** are for projects of limited

scope. They can be awkward to use and are better for organized storage than for active status.

- **Ring binders,** possibly with clear plastic pocket inserts, are a useful alternative for filing things, both active and for storage.
- **Electronic files** in your computer are superior to paper-based files when you need to store the data but don't need a hard copy to carry around or to give to others. They're also easy to access and can be turned into hard copy quickly. Perhaps best is that they can be discarded when you no longer need them, with just a click of the *delete* key.

More crucial than location is how your file is subdivided. There are four major alternatives:

- Alphabetical
- Topical
- Numerical
- Chronological

Each boasts its own particular strengths and weaknesses. Allow your instincts to guide you in deciding which suits your work or household management style. Remember: hybrid systems that combine two approaches often work best. A perfect example of this is the old Dewey Decimal system, a library cataloging system that groups books first according to subject matter, then alphabetically by author. The Library of Congress system employs the same basic principle.

The Ultimate Tool: Your Environment

Your desk, chair, file cabinets, shelving, walls—all these items make up an overall tool: your work environment. An efficient environment makes you much more productive, while an inefficient or uncomfortable one can eat into your time.

Yet few environments can seem more inflexible and beyond your control than the place where you work—unless, of course,

TOOLS

Filing Tips

Here are some ideas, options, and principles you may want to follow as you organize or reorganize your files. As you read, check the ones that work, or would work, best for you.

- ❑ Caption files with brief, simple phrasing.
- ❑ Begin each label phrase with a noun, followed by its description. It is similar to the library classification system: "correspondence—interoffice" is easier to find than "interoffice correspondence."
- ❑ If you are particularly aware of color, color coding or using little color dots on file tabs is a fine way to signal major filing categories.
- ❑ Transparent plastic folders or envelopes (which also come in colors) are useful as subdivisions within a folder since their contents are immediately identifiable.
- ❑ Never over-subdivide a single file slot. When there are several items or thicker documents (e.g., a book, printout, or report), use an accordion, flat-bottomed folder. If too many items begin to appear in a single file, it may be time to subdivide them into their own file categories or establish a new filing system.
- ❑ If a number of documents go in one folder (e.g., letters received at different times), slip the most recent one in front of the others. They will then be in reverse chronological order.
- ❑ If you take a critical document out for an extended period of time, leave a slip of paper or Post-it® to remind you that it is gone and where it went.
- ❑ Paper-clipped documents get confused in a file. The clips fall off or attach to something else. Staple such items together. If stapling would mutilate them, use a clear plastic folder or spring clamp to keep them together.
- ❑ Hanging folders are superior tools. The alternative causes overly-compact bunching, slipping into the bottom of the file cabinet, and so on. Most people do not actually use the hanging folder for direct storage but as a pocket for regular folders.
- ❑ Legal-size files are superior to letter-sized ones for this reason: something longer than 11 inches will not fit in a letter-sized file; almost any size will fit in an 8½ by 14-inch legal folder. So consider whether you will need these larger files.

- ❑ Binders that hang on a file suspension frame are an excellent alternative to shelf clutter.
- ❑ Invest in a high-quality labeling device to bring professionalism and conformity to your tabs and labels.
- ❑ At least once a month, devote an hour to thinning your in-desk files. Pay particular attention to any folder than appears overstuffed.
- ❑ Once every six months, purge all your active files of out-of-date information. Move legally necessary documents to storage. While there, check to see if anything has expired and throw them out. All other useless documents should be put into the recycle bin.

you're self-employed or the company president. Someone else probably dictates the color scheme, basic desk layout, and equipment. If you're lucky, you can add a photo of a loved one, bring in a desk lamp, or hang a painting of your choice. Odds are, though, that the more "corporate" your company is, the fewer choices you can make.

The most efficient and supportive work environment should include:

- A chair that is comfortable and ergonomic: it should support your posture and not cause back or neck fatigue.
- Lighting that's bright and that doesn't cast shadows where you most frequently work.
- Equipment that doesn't crowd your "free" workspace.
- The ability to access active materials without going too far.
- Soothing colors.
- No excessive noise.
- A location outside of traffic areas (unless it's your job to deal with those people).
- A window.
- Work surfaces that are clear of dust, dirt, etc.
- A comfortable and constant temperature in the room.

If your work environment has seven or more of these items,

Smart Managing

Balance Efficient and Effective

Must we always cram a maximum number of tasks into the time that's allotted to us? No, says Tom DeMarco, author of *Slack: Getting Past Burnout, Busywork, and the Myth of Total Efficiency*. DeMarco argues that total efficiency may make sense in a factory environment. But our economy depends much more on *knowledge* workers, who must have "slack" time to mentally prepare for work and to conceptualize new and valuable ideas. DeMarco concludes that by sacrificing efficiency a bit, you can make yourself and those you manage far more effective.

you have an ideal work environment. If it has fewer than five, your environment may be seriously subverting your efforts at efficiency and productivity. You need to find ways to improve your workspace.

If you enjoy considerable control over your work environment, you should find it easy, with commitment, to reshape it for maximum success. If not, consider the following:

- Keep your eyes open for a vacated workspace that would be better for you.
- Volunteer for a "work environment committee" or start one.
- Discuss possible changes in your work conditions with your boss. With worker's compensation lawsuits on the rise, companies are becoming much more willing to respond to such concerns.
- If all else fails, get permission to bring in your own chair, lamp, paint your walls, etc.

Conclusion

Having the right tools to manage your time is just one piece in the overall puzzle. The other pieces—prioritizing, dealing with procrastination, carving out blocks of time, delegating effectively, anticipating challenges, learning when to say no, and eliminating time leaks—can be effective in helping you to achieve your time management goals.

I hope that these general strategies and the practical tactics I've shared with you help put you on the road to a more productive, serene, and organizationally graceful life, one that fits your preferred approach to work and life.

Good luck in your efforts! You *can* succeed. Time needn't be your enemy. In fact, with the right techniques and tools, you can agree with the words of poet Sara Teasdale: "Time is a kind friend."

Manager's Checklist for Chapter 10

- ❑ Before selecting a timesaving tool, assess how its features fit your needs.
- ❑ Make sure it's user-friendly and reliable, and it will remain up-to-date for a reasonable length of time.
- ❑ Arrange your files for logic, ease, and instant accessibility.
- ❑ Shape your work environment for maximum pleasure and productivity.

Index